Praise for
Three Permissions

"The only way out of a tough spot is through it, and Robyn's book helps us to do just that. I love the metaphor of a permission slip. This book comes at a perfect time when we need resilience and strategies for coping with so much change—a practical and useful approach to navigating what's next in your life."

—**BRENDA ABDILLA,** PCC, author of *Outsmarting Crazytown*

"This, my friend, is not just a book, but a road map and lighthouse to those daring to step onto their paths of greatness! Life doesn't come with a manual. Even when we think we've figured it all out, unexpected moments remind us that we're not here to have all the answers but to explore, learn, and grow continuously. At its core, the book introduces the 'power of permission'—the act of giving yourself the authority to move forward without waiting for validation from others. You'll discover clear, actionable strategies to overcome self-doubt, challenge limiting beliefs, and make decisions that shape both your career and personal life. *Three Permissions* invites you to unlock the potential you already possess and embrace life as an ongoing adventure where you continuously evolve in the most authentic way possible."

—**SABINE GEDEON,** PCC, CPC, author of *LeadHership Reloaded*

"*Three Permissions* is a compelling and refreshing guide for anyone seeking to lead with greater authenticity, resilience, and emotional intelligence. Robyn invites readers on a deeply human journey—one that feels both personal and grounded in real-world insight. While many speak about success, few address the emotional complexity and inevitable failures along the way. This book brings those essential conversations to the forefront, offering a practical, science-backed framework for meaningful and lasting self-leadership."

—**JILL IPPOLITO,** professional coach

THREE PERMISSIONS

*The Power of Allowing
Yourself to Feel, Fail, and Fly
on the Path to Success*

ROBYN WHITE

All client anecdotes are amalgamations of multiple clients, to protect their privacy.

Published by River Grove Books
Austin, TX
www.rivergrovebooks.com

Copyright © 2025 Robyn White

All rights reserved.

Thank you for purchasing an authorized edition of this book and for complying with copyright law. No part of this book may be reproduced, stored in a retrieval system, or transmitted by any means, electronic, mechanical, photocopying, recording, or otherwise, without written permission from the copyright holder.

Distributed by River Grove Books

Design and composition by Greenleaf Book Group and Kim Lance
Cover design by Greenleaf Book Group and Kim Lance

Publisher's Cataloging-in-Publication data is available.

Print ISBN: 978-1-63299-954-2

eBook ISBN: 978-1-63299-955-9

First Edition

Dedicated to the memories of:

OLIVE HOLCOMB FEIGEL, 1894–1986

LOIS FEIGEL PARSONS, 1923–2020

SHERYL PARSONS SMITH, 1944–2023

Thank you for a beautiful legacy of strength, faith, and love.

CONTENTS

INTRODUCTION
Tap into the Power of Permission   1

PART I
PERMISSION TO FEEL   11

CHAPTER ONE
Planning to Feel: Feelings Map   13

CHAPTER TWO
Challenges to Permission to Feel   23

CHAPTER THREE
Feel Better   41

CHAPTER FOUR
Your Superpower of Mixed Emotions   55

CHAPTER FIVE
Practicing the Permission to Feel   69

PART II
PERMISSION TO FAIL   77

CHAPTER SIX
Planning to Fail: Failing Map   79

CHAPTER SEVEN
The Stumbling Blocks of Failure   93

CHAPTER EIGHT
Fail Better   111

Chapter Nine
Leveraging the Lessons of Failure   119

Chapter Ten
Practicing the Permission to Fail   129

Part III
Permission to Fly   141

Chapter Eleven
Planning to Fly: Flying Map   143

Chapter Twelve
Gravity and Drag of Flight   147

Chapter Thirteen
Fly Better   167

Chapter Fourteen
Flight Plan for Liftoff   185

Chapter Fifteen
Practicing the Principles of Flying   203

Next Steps
The Continuing Practice of Permission   233

Recommended Resources   237

Acknowledgments   239

Appendix 1: Emotions Thesaurus   241

Appendix 2: Readers' Guide   259

Notes   263

About the Author   267

TOOLS AND TEMPLATES

INTRODUCTION
    Three Bucket Theory   6

PART I: PERMISSION TO FEEL
    Permission to Feel Map   14
    Self-Assessment: Blame Response Scale   26
    Self-Trust Spectrum   27
    Self-Talk Endearment Practice   29
    Passivity Scale Self-Assessment   33
    Kind Assertiveness Practice   35
    Feel Better Permission Slip   41
    The Feelings Wheel   46
    Emotional Literacy Tracker   46
    Library of Emotions   49
    Feelings Power Pyramid   56
    FETBO Template   61
    Permission to Feel Self-Assessment   71
    Reflection Habit Questions   74

PART II: PERMISSION TO FAIL
    Permission to Fail Map   79
    Failure Inventory   90
    VIP Exercise   102
    Failure/Success Analysis Tool   122
    FETBO Template to Fail Better   130

Part III: Permission to Fly

    Permission to Fly Map   143

    FETBO Template and Self-Trust   156

    ANTs and MATs   158

    Dream Practice   168

    Dream List   174

    The So Method   176

    Dream Impact Zone   179

    Failure/Success Analysis for Flight Pre-Sight   186

    Flight Plan SMART Goals   196

    Beliefs Pre-Flight Check   209

    Beliefs Collective   222

    Permission to Fly Assessment   228

Next Steps:
The Continuing Practice of Permission

    Permission Practice Reflection Chart   234

○ Throughout the book, you will see this icon to signify tools and resources to build skills and awareness. Some readers may stop and do the exercises as they come in the pages, and some may want to return to the exercises later. Let the icons be a trail sign on your journey. You can also find digital versions of many of the exercises at the following QR code.

INTRODUCTION

Tap into the Power of Permission

You have permission to be here. In these pages, you are chosen, authorized, and purposed to show up in your life with authenticity and impact. Think about it: There are not very many scenarios in our adult lives where we are given permission to show up for ourselves. In fact, every day we are beset with expectations, obligations, and demands to show up for others, often to the exclusion of ourselves. As a result, conferring this permission to show up for yourself can be a very powerful tool—if you can learn to receive it.

What is it about permission that feels empowering? Do you remember the last time you had it? Probably sometime between the ages of eight and thirteen, you ambled confidently down a polished linoleum hall at your school, brandishing a hall pass from your teacher. You peek in the doors of other classrooms, inspiring jealousy among friends still bound by the grind of classwork, your steps echoing proudly through the hall's emptiness. No authorities were watching or telling you what to do in that moment. Or maybe you rushed, so filled with the import of your errand, the cadence of your shoes squeaking out your privilege. Remember the feeling of freedom, pride, boldness, and purpose?

Even if this anecdote doesn't ring true to your particular elementary school memories, you've no doubt had some variation of this experience where you were called upon and authorized to go on your own to a normally off-limits place with the excuse of a specific task. Those feelings, the agency, the confidence, the focus of your mission—that is what the power of permission is like.

But let's be clear, there are many different kinds of power. For the purposes of our work here, let's delineate two kinds of power: **(1) the power to influence or control others;** and **(2) the power to do what you want**, also called **autonomy**. Many studies have been done comparing these two kinds of power, and notably, as autonomy (power over yourself) increases, the drive for power (control) over others diminishes.[1] In a very measurable way, the fact is that autonomy wins.

That shouldn't be too surprising. We, as humans, highly value the ability to have power over ourselves—to feel that we have the confidence, freedom, and agency to live with purpose and genuine authenticity. But here's the thing: We don't realize the extent to which we are sometimes *our own greatest obstacle* to having the kind of autonomy we desire. For all sorts of reasons we will unpack shortly, you likely don't know how to truly grant yourself permission to lead yourself and exercise your own autonomy. But this is crucial if you want to feel emotionally fit, to show up with authenticity, and to create a meaningful impact for yourself and others. This book is designed to help you develop an awareness of emotional wellness, to build your emotional muscles, and to grant yourself permission in three key areas of self-leadership:

1. **Feeling**: Recognizing, allowing, processing, and valuing all your emotions
2. **Failing**: Learning from failure and leveraging your feelings about it
3. **Flying**: Taking action to attain your desired results, even surpassing your ideas of success

Feelings, failure, and flying (success) are common themes in my client work as an executive coach and life coach. I've seen that my clients' greatest hindrances in these areas are most often not caused by their circumstances or the people around them, but by themselves. The thoughts you allow yourself to think, the emotions you permit yourself to feel, and the actions you do or don't take are what define the impact of your life on others in the world around you. You are a human with limitless potential who, when given permission, can create such depth and width and breadth of influence for good. It's a travesty to withhold that permission from yourself—and yet so many of us do. So, how can you wrap your mind around the idea that it is not some outside force denying you authorization and autonomy? Because the truth is, it's you.

Before we go any further, let's define "permission" within the context of all this. For the purposes of this book, **permission is the understanding that you have the authority to move forward from your current state.** It's recognizing that you can grant yourself agency and practice the kind of self-leadership that allows you to live at your fullest potential. The opposite of permission is prohibition or forbidding a change from your current state. When you are in a state of prohibition, you're stuck living at less than you're capable of.

When you were a kid, you received the authority you needed from others, but you had very little autonomy. But what happens when you have autonomy as an adult and you want to create a meaningful, impactful life? Well, from what I've seen in my work, most people simply wait. They wait when they anticipate discomfort; they wait until they believe for certain that they'll get it right; they wait in case someone finds out they don't actually *deserve* the success they've "lucked" into. Sound familiar? Unfortunately, all this waiting will do is cause you to miss out on the richness that the full range of your own feelings can bring to your life. You will miss the lessons you can learn from not getting it right. You will miss relishing the success and satisfaction that come from generating the kind of impact you feel you were created for. When you wait, you abdicate the power of your autonomy and self-authority.

Sometimes, deference to the authority of others can become so habitual that you don't even notice you still have choices. You abide by the laws of society, operating within the company guidelines in your workplace, obeying your superiors, and following all of the unspoken rules and conventions around you. But every one of these circumstances offers a choice. Are there consequences to your choices? Absolutely. You can live peaceably or go to jail, you can work for that company or get fired, you can conform to others' standards or be shunned. You have choices about everything you do and waiting for permission leaves you in a holding pattern, destined for inaction. Over time, you find that you are not at all the person you want to be.

The three permissions I'll teach you in this book can release you from that holding pattern and free you to create amazing results in your life. Waiting for permission from others can make you passive. By giving yourself permission, you empower yourself to explore and embrace proactivity, even when it's uncomfortable. I invite you to stop waiting. Give yourself permission to feel, to fail, and to fly. You write the permission slip that helps you move forward into uncertainty with confidence, leverage and learn from failure, internalize success, and keep creating the impact you feel called to make. Stop waiting.

In the many clients and students I've worked with over the years, I've observed that there is almost always a reason why a person is withholding permission from themselves. Sometimes, people are victims of their feelings, or they are so shackled by their beliefs about a previous failure that their current actions are focused more on those past things than on healthy, productive, forward movements. They limit themselves, not realizing they've stopped reaching toward their goals. In other cases, they work themselves to the point of burnout to try to prove to themselves and others that they deserve their success. People stuck in these holding patterns stop creating impact—at least the impact they want. The work my clients and I do together has inspired these pages. I firmly believe that you can discover how to exercise your autonomy and re-establish your own authority to build a healthy relationship with your emotions, leverage failures to move forward authentically, and internalize success to create a life of impact. Don't misunderstand me, though, this will take work. Emotional challenges are part of being human, and they are hard stuff. But take heart—the struggles point to a better way to live.

Still not sure if this work is worth doing? Can you find yourself in any element of what we've discussed so far? Are you someone who doesn't feel like you experience or express emotions as easily as others around you? Do you find yourself limiting your interactions to avoid the consequences of uncomfortable emotions? Are you a person who works so hard to do everything perfectly and get ahead but constantly feel like your efforts aren't moving you forward? Are you so worried about taking a misstep that you are paralyzed into inaction? Have you already achieved some of your goals, perhaps even sooner than you expected, but you lay your head on the pillow at night wondering if you've done enough? Do you wake in the morning concerned that this might be the day everyone finds out you really don't know what you are doing? If any of this resonates with you, I want to assure you that you can understand yourself and your emotions better and live more effectively by tapping into the power of permission.

To be clear, you have control. You *own* control. Over the years, I've used the Three Bucket Theory to show my clients how to sort out what they can control and influence in their lives. The best I can tell, it originally comes from financial strategy planning, but I've always personally found it to be an effective tool that can be applied to the idea of self-leadership. **The Three Bucket Theory is simple: The circumstances of your life can be sorted into three buckets—things you can control, things you can influence, and everything else that doesn't fit into either of the first two buckets.**

The act of waiting for permission is basically taking something that belongs in your control bucket and putting it into another bucket. And it goes both ways: Sometimes, you may give yourself permission to take something that belongs in your influence or other bucket and put it in your control bucket. Keep this picture in mind as you do this work. People with permission are active stewards of what's in their buckets.

Where do you want to spend your time, energy, and focus?
It's your choice.

Image 0.1: Three Bucket Theory

HOW TO USE THIS BOOK

Three Permissions provides you with learnable maps to guide you through your journey of permission. When you do the work of letting yourself feel, fail, and fly, leveraging these key areas of self-leadership in your life, you create the kind of momentum you need for reaching your goals, feeling your best, and operating at a high level. In the coming pages, I'll share with you some of the most practical, achievable, and actionable tools I use with my clients, offering life-coaching in book form. You'll gain tools to understand how to develop better emotional fitness in work and life and how to manage yourself well to achieve what you want, live better, and make an impact. I'll show you how to adjust the emotions, mindsets, habits, and patterns that get in the way of your plans, so you can choose which emotions to feed, understand how to hold mixed emotions, and step into your authority. This book is your hands-on approach to self-leadership and emotional fitness.

In **Part I, Permission to Feel,** you will deepen your knowledge about emotions to build the foundation you'll need for the later chapters in the book. The feelings chapters are filled with practical applications, stories, and illustrations. You'll notice that this is the heftiest section of the book because understanding these concepts is essential to practicing permission. When you build the foundation of a proactive relationship with your emotions, you'll develop the confidence, competence, and capacity you'll need to deal with the challenges that often accompany the maps for both the failure and success (flight) sections of the book. In Permission to Feel, you'll explore skills and tools that show you how to handle and learn from both comfortable and uncomfortable feelings. You'll learn about self-trust and be equipped with methods to build that trust.

In **Part II, Permission to Fail,** you'll build your knowledge about failure. I'll show you how to process the difficult emotions that accompany failure and how you can recognize and leverage the knowledge that can be gleaned when you give yourself permission to fail.

And finally, in **Part III, Permission to Fly,** you'll look at flying—succeeding—and what permission to create impact can do to support you as you seek and sustain success.

While we talk about mindset throughout these pages, each permission begins with a Mission Mindset so that you know from the start what to expect and what mindset is needed for that particular permission. Don't worry if the Mission Mindset feels out of reach at the beginning; the work you do in each permission will help you adapt and embrace what you need.

With your efforts in these pages, you will recognize where you are withholding permission. This can be tricky, because you may grant yourself permission in specific areas or to a certain degree before putting on the brakes and denying yourself access. So how can you tell?

This book will help you develop awareness of those areas you have marked off-limits. You'll learn about barriers that block us from tapping into the power of permission, including lack of knowledge (self and otherwise), lack of tools, and lack of trust. Together, we will work with tools to help you develop the skills needed to support the return of that feeling you had, confidently walking the halls at school, fueled by the power of permission. The squeaky shoes? Well, that's up to you.

You have so much potential. I'm guessing, however, since you've picked up this book, that you or someone you love feels like life is falling short of expectations. Together, in these pages, you and I are going to explore and support three areas of the human experience that are rife with unfulfilled potential and inaccurate expectations. This is an educational book, a workbook, a guide.

When I hold this kind of book in my hand, I know I will spend a lot of time here. But that's me. If you want to skim the book or check out the map at the beginning of each section to see what catches your eye before jumping in, go for it. If you want to read this book and underline the things that resonate with you for future reference, do it. If you want to take a section and do each exercise in order, make it happen. It is designed for all these uses. However you approach this important work, I'm so proud of you for taking it on.

You'll see this many times in the pages you are about to turn: *Awareness is the beginning of all work*. Whether you skim or deep dive, you're creating awareness. Similar to a workout, the more time, repetitions, and weight you commit to, the more defined your results will be. You may not want to be on the cover of *Muscle & Fitness* magazine. Maybe you're looking for functional fitness. Or perhaps you want energy and movement but don't want to invest in a lot of muscle-defining exercises. Any of these objectives is just fine. If you do the work, you will create awareness that brings results.

I want to take a quick moment to talk about our relationship. I have given considerable thought to you, my reader. We are going to spend significant time together in these pages. Many of the things we talk about are based on my own experiences and my clients' experiences. The advantage of working with clients over trying to engage with readers is, my clients teach me about themselves; I am their coach and guide, but they are the experts on themselves. I have attempted to anticipate your questions, but I want you to feel empowered here, not judged or condescended to. I am in this with you, learning about this human experience as I navigate my journey. The examples in this book, though they are framed as singular client stories, are actually amalgamations of multiple clients. I've done this both to protect my clients' privacy and to avoid example overload while exploring the themes common in my clients' work. I am grateful to the clients who have allowed me to walk alongside them in their journeys, because not only is it fulfilling work, but it also brings out the treasures of their stories and lessons learned that I can apply in my own life and bring together for others. That's what we are doing here—collectively moving forward as each of us individually moves forward.

Thank you for choosing to invest your time in this work. Feel empowered to try the steps captured for you here, grab hold of the bits that are most helpful, and jettison anything that doesn't serve you. Then share the tools and practices that helped you so that others can move forward, too. I'm sending you so much thought and love as we get started.

The last thing I want you to keep in mind before we begin is this: To be able to implement your permissions most effectively as you practice the concepts in this book, you'll need to learn how to **approach**, **adjust**, and **act** in each instance. These verbs are principles you and I will leverage to unpack each element of our three permissions. It means first prioritizing your choice to get close to and spend time with your experiences, feelings, and thoughts. Then, you may open yourself up to changing your thoughts, feelings, and strategies. Finally, you will be able to intentionally choose and implement action over inaction.

You will start noticing these principles at play as we move forward. In each section of the book, I will note how our work is based on these three principles. However, you can already start noticing these principles in your daily life by asking a few simple questions of yourself: Am I approaching or avoiding this thought, feeling, or experience? Am I willing to adjust my thinking, feeling, or acting here? Am I moving to intentionally act based on my strategy here or settling for inaction (deciding later)?

Now, I'm picturing you reaching this point in the book as if you were unfolding a map and looking at the legend to get your bearings. Take a deep breath, and remember you have permission to be here. Let's get started!

PART I

Permission to Feel

Mission Mindset: Feelings are **partners** providing vibrancy and information.

Why emotions first? Regardless of the resulting success or failure, in attempting to reach goals, you will contend with emotion. Emotional wrestling is energy-zapping. But when you have the knowledge and the skills to process and even leverage emotions to move yourself forward, you can funnel more energy into your actions and create greater impact at an accelerated pace. Odds are, like me, you experience feelings that discourage and demotivate when things aren't going well. You may also struggle with uncomfortable feelings when things do go well even if you're not aware of it. Many people struggle with internalizing success. In my experience, if you don't understand how to give yourself permission to feel, you will miss the value of failure, short-circuit the momentum of success, and diminish the richness of the human experience.

Most likely you are not afraid of or disinterested in taking actions toward your goals, or you would not have picked up this book. But honestly, there is very little risk in opening a book. Actions that lead to real failure or success tend to be more challenging because they could leave you vulnerable to the emotions that are their traveling companions—uncertainty, dread, shame, regret, and discomfort. You may ask, "Okay, I get that with failure, but why would I avoid the emotions that accompany success?" While joy, exhilaration, and satisfaction are most commonly associated with success, there are others as well: dread of losing those desirable emotions, fear that you haven't earned the right to experience those emotions, worry over peaking and never experiencing them again, and overwhelm with the effort of trying to sustain the desirable feelings. Because feelings can be powerful drivers of behavior, building feelings fitness supports your work in the mindset and actions of both failure and success.

Part I of this book demonstrates how feelings can be triggers of action and inaction. When you learn to build feelings fitness—to partner with them—you will be strengthened by your ability to create supportive mindsets and take informed and intentional actions toward success. I will show you how to gain knowledge of and awareness about your emotions and employ tools to help you achieve the results you want. I believe the most important tool is not one found in the typical toolbox—it is a blueprint. In the coming chapters, I will walk you through the **Permission to Feel Map**, a blueprint for understanding your emotions that can transform the way you think, feel, and act.

Planning to Feel: Feelings Map

have a friend who once challenged herself to hike solo across the bottom of the Grand Canyon, rim-to-rim, in one day. Before her journey, she did a lot of research, studying the routes and gathering information from people who had taken the trail before her, so she could learn from their experiences. My friend was already in good shape but trained heavily before her hike in order to make sure she was physically prepared. She also made sure to acquire the right tools for the job, including a backpack for her supplies, the right kind of hiking boots, and a customized map. The thought and effort she put into this preparation didn't result in a hike that was completely free from challenges—even unanticipated ones—but preparing herself this way did set her up for a successful endeavor.

In much the same way, while the challenges of your own journey may not be physical like a hike across the Grand Canyon, they will demand energy, intention, and consistent focus. To build literacy around your feelings and have a healthy relationship with your emotions so you can live with more impact, you need to stay invested and engaged. If you follow the path laid out in this book, you will be building emotional muscle so that no matter what your current condition, you will reap benefits from this work.

As you journey through these pages, you will likely experience both familiar and unfamiliar landmarks. You will develop new perspectives as you grow in your ability to tap into the power of permission for the trip. You'll notice that the Permission to Feel Map looks a bit like a mountain, and I invite you to think of it as such. You're beginning your journey by climbing a mountain and, as most mountain climbing goes, you'll start at the bottom and work your way up—and it will be *work*. No worries, though. While giving permission and committing to a long journey can be daunting, you'll be able to take it at a good pace with rest stops of reflection and snacks of success.

A MAP FOR YOUR JOURNEY

As you work your way through each of the permissions, I'd like you to play your own version of *Where's Waldo?* Throw on your striped shirt and glasses and with each step, observe where *you* are. While I will guide you on this journey according to where you are in the book, I encourage you to take note of where you are in your personal permissions journey. At various points along your journey, I will ask you to measure your progress with the tools provided. Ready to check out the Permission to Feel Map? Let's go.

Image 1.1: Permission to Feel Map

The Permission to Feel Map can be used to orient you on your journey through this work. It presents a linear path for the journey. However, you are unique and will process this information through your own lenses. So go ahead, exercise your permission muscle and let yourself travel this route at your own pace, moving through the process at a high level or setting up camp for a deep dive into an area that challenges you. In life, you are often asked to take courage and motivation from a clear vision of your end goal with very little knowledge of the steps it will take to get there. This Permission to Feel Map will offer you both.

Take a minute and turn your attention to the end goal of the feelings journey, which I call feelings fitness. For the purposes of this book, the words "emotions" and "feelings" are used interchangeably. In academic circles, they are delineated for good reasons, but discussions here will be limited to practical applications of general concepts. Additionally, "fitness" can also be described as a state of being "sound," "equipped," and "ready." Focus on what feelings fitness means to you. What would it do for you to think of your emotions and have these words—sound, equipped, ready—come to mind? Let your shoulders relax and connect with the vision of yourself with feelings fitness. Now, study each step of the Permission to Feel Map, working backward from feelings fitness all the way until you reach the red arrow at the start. The feelings-fit version of yourself is calling you forward. All you have to do right now is keep reading.

EXPERIENCE YOUR EMOTIONS

A client of mine had been working with me during a time of transition as she was re-entering the workforce after a relocation and taking some time off to deal with a chronic health condition. Over the course of our last few sessions, she was super focused on what was next for her. She had done the work of developing tools to start building a support network and begin exploring her new work options. But she confessed to me that despite what we'd discussed in our last meeting, she hadn't pursued any of those resources. She said it had been a discouraging week, her health condition had a minor flare, and she'd had a conversation about retirement with her spouse that had led to her spiraling into sadness over not knowing how much her chronic illness would limit her future plans.

Her feelings and need for a pause were absolutely legitimate. But as her coach, I asked if we could explore if it was really battling the illness that was holding her back or, rather, if it was her fear of uncertainty that stopped her from pursuing her new network. She was a strong woman who was not settling for a victim mindset, so we got to work exploring her emotions and how they could be recognized and leveraged as a source of learning while moving forward toward her goals. My client was expending all of her energy wrestling her feelings, trying to distract from and even deny those that were most uncomfortable. This wrestling not only sapped her energy but also left her vulnerable to demotivating and discouraging thoughts that stopped her forward movement. She needed to reallocate her energy to allow all of her feelings and to focus emotional power into supporting her progress toward creating the life she wanted. She needed permission.

Take a minute and ask yourself this question: Am I feeling *all* of my feelings? You may have bought into the lie that you should feel happy all the time—and if you are not happy, you just need to try harder, accept that God doesn't like you, or that you're abnormal. Social media can perpetuate this lie because people only present a curated view of their lives: Everything is great, everyone loves me, I'm successful, my children are successful, I have the best dog, job, friends, hobbies, vacations, everything.

Hear this truth: We are created to experience all emotions. This is the human experience. No emotions, no humanity. Why do I believe this? First, because there are words in our language for all kinds of emotions, not just the happy, joyful ones. Second, because great writings that stir us are not the ones about characters who are happy all the time. When obstacles appear, these characters don't happily stop their hero's journey or smilingly leap over the obstacle and continue merrily on. A hero's journey is a hero's journey because heroes keep going, learning from and managing their emotions and experiences to work through, around, or over obstacles along the way. Third, I believe we are created to experience all emotions because emotions are powerful. They add richness to our lives—empowering our decision-making, our communication, and our connections.

I really enjoy word studies, meaning I like to track down the origin and meaning of words to better understand how to accurately apply them. The word "emotion," finds its etymology in the Latin, *emovere*, which means to disrupt or stir up. And isn't that what emotions do? Emotions are what keep you from sleeping through life. They stir you up! They are not always fun—in fact, sometimes they are poignantly painful. And sometimes they are wonderful and exhilarating in a way that is difficult to describe.

> **We are created to experience all emotions.**

EMOTIONS ARE TEACHERS

Some thirty-seven years ago, a man named Elliot came to the attention of noted neuroscientist and author Antonio Damasio. Earlier in his life, Elliot had a promising career in a business firm and great relationships with his siblings, his wife, and his children. By the time Elliot and Damasio met, Elliot had undergone brain surgery to remove a large tumor and some damaged brain tissue. He had recovered physically and could hold an engaging conversation about the day's news and recount his life story with fascinating detail. However,

> **Emotions are powerful. They add richness to our lives—empowering our decision-making, our communication, and our connections.**

he'd lost his job, his marriage had ended, and his other relationships were strained.

Damasio administered IQ tests and memory assessments to Elliot, whose performance was exemplary. However, when Damasio examined his patient's work performance, he noted that Elliot spent hours not working but trying to prioritize his work tasks, not actually able to decide where to start. Similarly, Elliot couldn't make social plans more than a couple of hours in advance.

Damasio determined that intellect was not the problem and began testing Elliot's responses to emotionally charged images. Elliot experienced these images as emotionally neutral. Damasio described Elliot's situation as knowing but not *feeling*. Damasio wrote, "I began to think that the cold-bloodedness of Elliot's reasoning prevented him from assigning different values to different options and made his decision-making landscape hopelessly flat." Elliot's lack of emotional value differentiation rendered him unable to evaluate different options or envision different scenarios when presented choices that needed to be made.[1]

Like Elliott, if you are without the ability to filter decisions through the lens of your emotions, you can become overwhelmed with options and stymied in decision-making. You do not need to suffer brain trauma to find yourself in a similar position. Emotions are teachers. But if you ignore, fight, or suppress feelings that you label "bad" or "negative," then you will miss out on the lessons they have to teach. The reality is that emotions cannot be classified as "good" and "bad." Each emotion provides valuable information that you must rely on to grow as a human. What kinds of valuable information? Data that can motivate you to act, help others understand how you perceive the world, support your ability to gather information about and relate to others, and aid you in decision-making.

This does not mean that you need to tell the world every feeling you experience. But you need to tell *yourself*. You must cultivate more literacy about your emotions, appreciate what they add to your life, glean what you can from their meaning, and leverage them to make this life full of inward meaning and outward impact.

CHANGE YOUR APPROACH TO EMOTIONS

What does permission have to do with this? Remember that permission means doing something with full authority and freedom. When you have authority and freedom to feel every emotion, you are able to not only experience life in technicolor but explore the *causes* of the emotion and exercise choice around how you want to act on it. You can even shift your emotion into one that serves you better. Even though I believe you are designed to experience every emotion, it is not beneficial to act on every emotion. Your goal is to experience every emotion and then *choose* how you want to respond, not to be blindly driven by your feelings.

> Emotions are teachers, but if you avoid them, you miss out on the lessons they offer.

Think about the process of dealing with feelings like digging a deep hole for a well. An uncomfortable emotion comes along, and you quickly toss it down the well and slap a cover on it. But this is only a temporary solution. Now you have a couple of options: either deny the existence of the hole or uncover it and start sorting through all of the stuff you've packed in there. Option one requires increasing energy, and it has a huge downside. Because you've indiscriminately thrown all emotions in this hole, you are now becoming incapable of discerning what is comfortable and what is uncomfortable. The effort and energy you spend on well-cover maintenance will exhaust you. The second option is to open the well and start to sort out the emotions. This will require so much time that you are likely to grow impatient and slap the lid back on as soon as you get enough space in your well to ease your anxiety.

The good news is that there is actually a third option: You can change the way you deal with emotions and do away with the well completely. Instead, exchange it for a Library of Emotions, which you can use to learn the lessons of emotions and choose the feeling that serves you best.

To accomplish this, you first must develop the skill of emotional literacy—a familiarity with and understanding of your own emotions. Even this step can incite trepidation, because you may by now be averse to uncomfortable feelings. Emotions don't create a physical injury that you can see on an X-ray, but your experience of them can feel just as—or sometimes even more—painful. That is why people often work so hard to avoid those uncomfortable feelings. Just as getting clarity about your own identity will help to develop your trust in yourself, identifying your emotions will help you learn to trust them.

For your work in this book, you will learn to conceptualize emotions as vibrations in your body that have a message for you. That's easy to say but harder to remember when you feel betrayed by someone you care about or grief after losing a loved one. But hanging on to this concept can help diminish the power of the feelings you deem negative. Applying this concept is just like developing muscle—it demands embracing discomfort and intentional focus, discipline, and consistency.

Before moving on, take a minute to reflect on what you understand so far about your plan to feel. What is new information for you? I realize you are at the very beginning of your work, and I don't want the next section to discourage you, but the most effective plans take into careful consideration what obstacles might be encountered. Acting on the principle of permission, we are empowering ourselves to **approach** feelings, **adjust** thinking about emotions, and plan strategic **actions** that will build emotional fitness. Even if you are already aware of some of these obstacles, this work will help you develop strategies and muscles to overcome them.

TAKEAWAYS

- **Giving yourself permission to feel is like climbing a mountain:** It requires a map to guide you, adequate preparation for the journey ahead, and commitment to following through when things get hard.
- Following the **Permission to Feel Map** can help you reach your end goal of feelings fitness.
- Feeling all of your emotions is central to the human experience, but **acting on those emotions is a conscious choice.**
- Building **emotional literacy** unlocks a **Library of Emotions,** empowering you to choose the ones that best serve you.
- Conceptualizing emotions as **vibrations in your body that have a message for you** can help diminish the power of uncomfortable feelings.

2

Challenges to Permission to Feel

By the time my friend finally undertook her solo hike of the Grand Canyon, she had put hours upon hours of preparation and planning into the trip. However, this preparation did not assure her an experience that was free from surprises. For example, it took her longer than she anticipated to make the distance, and it was fully dark by the time she climbed up out of the canyon—making for a more harrowing journey than expected. One of the challenges she *had* anticipated and planned for was food: first, having enough food for the day, and second, remembering to eat it.

There were camping lodges at a couple of places along the route where hikers could get snacks and refill water. But my friend had learned that hiking to those spots would require a lot of energy, as would the hike from either lodge out of the canyon. She opted to bear the extra weight and bulk in her pack to have enough food and water without relying on outside resources. As hikers expend energy and deal with the suffocating heat of summer in the Grand Canyon, they often do not feel like eating. To deal with this, my friend set an alarm on her watch to remind herself to eat. When the alarm sounded, she ate whether she wanted to or not. The alarm created awareness that she had a need and the resources to meet it.

No, this book is not about hiking the Grand Canyon, but as you give yourself permission to move through this journey, you can create awareness about and strategies for some of the challenges you must overcome. Not only *can* you, you *must*, or you will not make it through to the end. I know, you picked up the book to learn about the three permissions, and I promise you will learn to scale those mountains. But first, you must do the necessary prep work to ensure a strong finish. It's time to look at some of the challenges that keep you from building a healthy partnership with your emotions.

THE FOUR CHALLENGES

There are four specific challenges that will show up in each of your permissions on this journey: blame, self-trust, passivity, and identity. By the time you have completed your work, you will have new awareness of each of these obstacles and the skills to use the tools I will unpack for you. These tools will be presented for different challenges as you will find them in your journey, and I'll show you how to apply them at the right points along the way.

Blame

This is a sneaky challenge that I often help my clients create awareness around in their work to give themselves permission to feel. It comes up so often that I call it the blame response. The blame response is what it sounds like: a nearly involuntary thought process wherein you assign the cause of your feelings to forces outside of yourself. In psychology, this is known as having an external locus of control. The blame response gives the illusion of working because it functions like a protection guarantee. As long as your challenges are caused by someone or something else, then you don't have to feel bad about yourself or take responsibility for your feelings.

Do you often jump to point out how others are wrong around challenging circumstances? "If you'd only done x, y, z, then this wouldn't have happened." "If you'd kept track of your phone, then you wouldn't have wasted all that time looking for it and we wouldn't be late." If you're being honest with yourself, these statements rarely reflect the whole truth. For instance, if you look at your role in these circumstances, you might see that if you had stopped for gas on the way home last night as your partner had requested, you wouldn't have needed to spend time getting gas, which was the main contributor to being late, versus the few minutes your partner took looking for their phone. If you observe yourself adopting this kind of blame-shifting language when things don't turn out the way you want, then you are exercising the blame response. Do that often enough and it is more accurately classified as the blame habit.

If the negative effect you have on those around when you choose to blame them isn't enough motivation to change your approach, consider this: The blame response is an illusion that can trap you in your unwanted feelings and outcomes—because as long as your feelings are someone else's fault, you can't change them. What you own, you can alter. It's like the difference between renting an apartment and owning a house. In an apartment, most of the time, you can't paint the walls or renovate but you also don't have to fix the broken dishwasher or repair a leaky roof. As a homeowner, you can make any renovations or changes you want but you also have to deal with the upkeep.

> **What you own, you can alter.**

Similarly, ownership of your feelings can come with some discomfort, but it also comes with the power to change everything. A while back, I was meeting with a client I'll call Joe. We had been working together a few months when he came to the session so excited. I asked him what the source of his enthusiasm was, and he told me he had been practicing this process of approaching and adjusting his feelings to support actions that would move him toward his goals. "I feel like I can do anything if I take my time to work through this process. I guess I feel like I have discovered my superpower," he said. And he was right. This kind of work isn't a magic formula, and it won't create the same overnight transformation as, say, being bitten by a radioactive spider, but it *is* empowering. However, you can't do the work until you break the blame habit and, instead, own your feelings and the results you are creating in your life.

What does the blame habit have to do with not giving yourself permission? Remember the three areas of permission we're seeking: permission to feel, fail, and fly. When you blame, you are dodging your feelings. When you blame, you are disowning your failures. When you blame, you become blind to feedback that can help you fly.

PREPARE FOR THE CHALLENGE OF BLAME

So how do you stop the blame habit? At this point in your journey, I want you to create awareness about your blame response. Congratulations, you have already begun that work by reading and learning about it. Now it's time to notice it in your everyday life. Watch out for language such as, "If you'd just . . ." "What were you thinking?" "Well, if you hadn't . . ." "You made me feel . . ." Sometimes, you may use words that point at others in a legitimate way, but in order to notice the blame response, you will need to catch these words and look at what role you have in the feelings and outcomes you are experiencing. If you create awareness about the blame habit, that alone will change how often you lean on it to deal with uncomfortable emotion. You will do deeper work on this in your next permission. For now, create awareness. Remember—awareness is the beginning of all work.

At the end of each day, I recommend rating yourself on a scale of 1–10, with 1 being "I notice that I consistently used the blame response" and 10 being "I didn't use the blame response at all." At the end of the week, reflect on the following prompts by taking the time to journal about them:

- What have I learned about my relationship with blame?
- What kind of challenge does the blame habit present in my permission to feel?

Self-Trust

The second challenge on your permission to feel journey is self-trust. Let's be clear about the meaning of self-trust. It's not believing that you will always make the right choice, be physically able to do anything and everything, or never experience uncomfortable emotions. It is having faith that you will do the best you can to show up for yourself and others with respect and kindness—that you will choose actions that align with your values and goals.

Think of self-trust as existing on a spectrum. Keep in mind that you may have different levels of self-trust in different areas, thus supporting the idea that you give yourself more permission in some areas than in others. You can probably link the areas where you are denying permission to areas where you exercise low levels of self-trust. Take a look at the following:

- **Self-Trust:** Having the faith that you will do the best you can to show up for yourself and others with respect and kindness, no matter the result of your efforts, the circumstances, or what anyone else says.
- **Self-Doubt:** Lacking confidence in your ability to think, act, or feel in a way that's best for you and others.
- **Self-Abandonment:** Choosing not to meet a known personal need, honor your values, or pursue your goals.

I put them in a spectrum because a person high in self-trust rarely practices self-abandonment. Think about a friendship you've had where you trusted that person completely. They had your back, and you had theirs. Never would you abandon them in a struggle! A person high in self-trust has their own back. Think again about this friend that you trust. Imagine that they called you on the phone and told you their life partner had left them to be with someone else. Would you say, "Well, you know, you have been letting yourself go," "You're not as young as you used to be," "I've noticed you've put on some weight," "They probably just got tired of you and your issues, like I have," and then end the call? *No!* You would respond with, "I'm so sorry," "How are you feeling?" or "What can I do to help you through this?" Not abandonment, not judgment, but compassion.

When you show up compassionately for your friend, you build a trusting relationship with them. In the same way, when you show up compassionately for yourself, you build a trusting relationship with yourself. In educational psychologist Dr. Kristin Neff's work, she points to the value of self-compassion over self-esteem. Neff says, "The self-worth that comes from being kind to yourself is much more stable than that which comes from judging yourself positively."[1] Because I agree with Dr. Neff that self-compassion is a stable foundation for building self-trust and giving yourself permission, you will see opportunities to build self-compassion throughout your work in these pages.

How do you know where you fall on the Self-Trust Spectrum? Start with the approach. The first step is to create awareness about your self-trust, specifically in permission to feel. A person with high self-trust says, "I know I can handle uncomfortable feelings," "I know how to identify what I need in difficult circumstances and how to ask for it," "I can rely on myself to make good choices in self-care," "I trust my own opinions and know how to determine what I want," "When I commit to something, I know I will show up and give it my best," "My best doesn't have to be perfect," and "I understand my values and can hold my personal boundaries." If you identify with these statements in your words and thoughts, you are high in self-trust.

Conversely, a person with high self-doubt says, "I'm not sure how to figure out what I want," "I often seek others' opinions before I consider my own," "I am quick to point out my flaws before I notice my successes," "I work extra hard to create perfect results," and "I hold some boundaries and have a rough idea of what I value."

Finally, someone who is engaging in self-abandonment says, "My inner critic is sarcastic and quick to jump in," "I rarely know what I want or how to figure it out," " Even if I can identify them, I never state my own preferences," "I am elated with the praise of others and devastated by criticism," "I procrastinate about anything that I doubt I can do perfectly," and "What are boundaries?"

This is a simple self-assessment to help increase awareness. Again, you may find that in some areas of life, you are higher in self-trust than in others. Maybe at work, you know exactly what you want and can pursue it, regardless of the feelings that come up, but in relationships you struggle to believe you are worthy or to understand what you are looking for. That's okay—you are human, and you struggle with human things. For now, just notice these areas and the different levels of self-trust you hold in your life. Sometimes, creating awareness can bring up deflating emotions. That's normal. As I said at the beginning of this book, this work can be uncomfortable, and many areas will stretch you. That is how you build the muscle to give yourself permission. You are going to consistently work on self-trust throughout your journey. Awareness is the beginning.

PREPARE FOR THE CHALLENGE OF SELF-TRUST

As you continue to notice areas where you are not in high self-trust, let's use a tool to begin building this trust. Start with how you talk to yourself. Even if your self-talk is relatively kind, let's make it kinder by prefacing it with an internal endearment—sweetheart, love, darlin', or a nickname. This may feel awkward at first, but think about when you are in a loving relationship: Have you noticed certain endearments you use when speaking to that person? Do you remember an endearment someone has used for you?

I had a client who was beginning this journey, and she chose a term of endearment that her mother still uses with her, even as an adult. Because her mother was a big support on her journey, she chose that as a reminder of loving trust. I often use "Rob," which is my husband's nickname for me. Not long ago, one of my adult daughters let me know that I don't really use her childhood nickname, "Boodle," anymore, and she missed it. Using a term of endearment for yourself cues feelings of being cared for and belonging. While I have committed to using my daughter's nickname more often to cue those feelings for her, you can do the same for yourself by adding an endearment to your self-talk. This will start strengthening your self-trust with a foundation of self-compassion. What endearment will you use? How will you remember to use it?

Let me add that measurement matters. In case you haven't already noticed, throughout the book, I mention ways to measure your work. If you don't measure, how do you know you're progressing? For the aforementioned quick win, you could keep a tally on a sticky note or in the Notes app on your phone every time you remember to use your endearment. Or at the end of each day, you could check in and rate yourself on a scale of 1–10, with 1 being "I didn't use my endearment at all" and 10 being "That's the only way I address myself internally." Notice your numbers, and notice how your energy shifts as you grow in this practice.

> **Measurement matters.**

Passivity

A third challenge you may face in giving yourself permission is the practice of passivity. Passivity is often *rooted* in a lack of self-trust, but it is more than just lack of self-trust or confidence in your plans. It is instead an intentional strategy to avoid taking action. Passivity is defined by the APA Dictionary of Psychology as "a form of adaptation, or maladaptation, in which the individual adopts a pattern of submissiveness, dependence, and retreat into inaction."[2] A passive person views themselves as playing a supporting role in their own life movie—not as the writer, director, or even the star—and they are good with that. Surviving rather than thriving has become their comfort zone, not because it's cozy and warm but because it's predictable and safe.

Passive people often approach life longing to be rescued, hoping to win the lottery, or grunting and getting through it. Sometimes, they choose passivity not only because it's the path of least resistance, but because it feels less troublesome than upsetting or hurting others. People who practice passivity may feel that if they choose their own paths or stand up for themselves, someone else will be hurt, upset, or inconvenienced. Taking action that promotes their ideas, opinions, or goals feels selfish. They either don't see or don't recognize the possibility of a win-win resolution of conflict—the idea that someone will be unhappy with them is not worth the risk. Sometimes, to gain some control, someone practicing passivity may even verbally comply but actively undermine what they've agreed to.

Do you recognize these patterns in yourself? What we're talking about is a way of thinking that is holding you back from giving yourself permission to act and causing you to retreat into inaction. The passivity habit is tricky because it is an *unconscious* pattern of behavior. One reason passivity becomes habitual is because at some point (maybe even multiple points) in time, passivity worked. It rescued you, whether literally or figuratively, from uncomfortable feeling or even physical danger. And there *are* situations where passive behavior is the healthy choice. Refusing to be provoked by a bully, for instance, can be essential for maintaining your personal safety. Choosing not to speak until you've cooled off can be a beneficial approach to conflict. However, these are situational *choices* based on context. On the other hand, because of your experiences, your brain may have adopted passivity as a "tried and true" strategy to be applied in every situation it perceives as threatening. The problem here is that not all situations your brain classifies as threatening are actually a threat.

Passivity can also become a habit when it is easy—the path of least resistance. Perhaps you habitually base your choices on what's most pleasant, least painful, and least effortful. When it's easy, your brain, which likes to conserve energy and keep you on a predictable path, gives you a little pat on the back for passivity, in the form of the neurotransmitters dopamine and serotonin. Those neurotransmitters give us pleasure and comfort, which in turn tell your brains that passivity is a good strategy.

Sometimes, a passivity habit develops because it feels like the best way to receive the approval of others. As long as you do whatever is asked, maybe you won't be rejected. The passivity habit may also develop because you don't want to take responsibility for the results you are creating. If you took action and still didn't get what you wanted, then you would need to take accountability for your results. This form of passivity is a cousin of the blame habit fed by fear of failure or rejection.

Notice if any of these sound like you: "I could be wrong, but . . ." "If it's meant to be, it will be." "I don't want to be any trouble." "I really need to get home, but sure I can take you where you want to go." "I have a massive deadline, but I can take time to come help you." "Well, they are all good options, so you choose." "I don't care." "I don't know." If these statements show up frequently in your day-to-day interactions, you might be practicing passivity.

Using qualifying speech *can* be a way to be diplomatic, but if you use it every time you express an opinion, it could be because you don't want action taken based on the opinion you are expressing. The practice of passivity can also show up in soft-spokenness and a slow pace (but not always—some of us are wired to be soft spoken and process thoughts into words at a different pace). You can tell the difference between hard-wired characteristics and passive practice by noticing the goal of the behavior. As a passive practice, you do it hoping to create time for someone else to choose a path for you. This strategy strives to keep you in your comfort zone as much as possible.

Your comfort zone is not always comfortable, but it is always predictable. Once again, this is something your brain likes. What is predictable is not a threat, and that must mean it's a safe space to stay alive. However, growth happens in unpredictability. It happens outside the comfort zone. If you want to grow and change things about your life, you have to embrace the idea of being uncomfortable for a bit. While your brain will resist stepping out of this zone, you get to boss your brain—because you have the authority to grant permission.

PREPARE FOR THE CHALLENGE OF PASSIVITY

Passivity can be called for in certain situations, but when it moves into the realm of habit, then you're not even choosing. You've just relinquished your power in all situations, and you don't even notice anymore. Grow your awareness of your passive tendencies and use it to step into your autonomy and reclaim your right to choose.

Take a few days to observe your behavior. Give yourself a score on a daily passivity scale and see where you land. Zero on the scale is: "I make decisions or at least take steps toward them," "I do most tasks immediately or assign them a time, show up at that time, and get them done," "I may consider a few people's opinions, but I decide for myself and act accordingly," and "I know that learning, intention, and support can and do change any thoughts and behavior." On the other end of the scale, a 10 would be: "I struggle hourly to make any decision with which I'm faced," "I regularly put off less desirable tasks. They pile up and I try not to think about them," "I'm constantly seeking other people's opinions and often choose things and activities just because someone else says to," "I am set in my ways," and "I never change or deviate from my norm. I tell myself and others, 'That's just the way I am.'"

Do this for a few days, and you should have a pretty clear picture of your passivity levels. As I'm writing this, I feel like I'm coming down hard on passive types. We all have times when passivity shows up. As long as it's not a regularly repeated behavior pattern and you are only choosing to be passive once in a while in appropriate circumstances, it's probably not much of an obstacle to giving yourself permission. Those who practice passivity regularly either don't realize it or do—and like it.

In creating this awareness, you'll recognize which category you fit into and can commit to start changing. Now that you've noticed, you can start creating change with learning, intention, and support. To aid you in doing the work, here are some power principles for breaking the passivity habit:

- **Don't wait for motivation to get moving**: Action leads to motivation, not the other way around. If you adopt that way of thinking, you exercise influence instead of relying on the influence of others. You're not at the mercy of when motivation shows up.

- **Momentum steps matter**: Choosing quick-win actions helps you build momentum to keep being proactive.

- **Meaningful goals matter**: Choosing goals that stretch you, align with your values, and get you out of your comfort zone will not accommodate passivity.

- **Paralysis by analysis is real**: Being able to analyze a situation and plan a response are helpful skills, but overdoing either is passive behavior. Endless researching is passive behavior disguised as active behavior—being busy but not taking action.

- **Passivity is different than creating margin**: Like in art or writing, the blank space or a patch of uncolored canvas in life is there to give you a break. It is empty, restful time to recharge. I like how Michael Hyatt defines it as "the space between our load and our limit."³ Creating margin is not a passive endeavor. It takes intention, purpose, and self-advocacy to protect the white space in your life.

I'm going to list a few steps to help you break the pattern of passivity, but also remember that you are just priming the permission pump here in this first section of the book. As you work through the permission process in the other areas, you will be taking action and breaking the power of the passivity habit.

- **Kind assertiveness**: Practice expressing your ideas, beliefs, and opinions in a non-judgmental, respectful way.
- **Keep your vision in mind**: Regularly seek clarity and remind yourself of how you want to show up, where you want to go, what you need, and what gives you energy.
- **Insert your values**: Clarify your top values and notice how your choices honor, compromise, or disassociate with those values.
- **Notice your emotions and physiology**: Acknowledge and name your emotions. Deep breathe to calm your responses to the circumstance.
- **Declare and deliver**: Declare your appreciation for the person and their perspective and deliver your opinion or approach or boundary. A few notes on delivery: Own your opinion ("My opinion is . . ."), choose your approach wisely, consisting of one of the following:
    - **Agreement**: Only agree if you can do it with joy and it aligns with your values and vision.
    - **Compromise**: Partial agreement that supports you and the other party.

- **Offering alternatives:** Help explore other options that support both you and the other party.
- **Disagree:** State your disagreement about the issue, not the person with whom you are disagreeing, and be at peace with yourself.

Let's practice stepping just the tiniest bit out of the comfort zone that passivity provides. For the next week, challenge yourself to give your opinion first in a group setting. You don't have to offer an opinion when it isn't requested and relevant to the situation. However, when your work crew is trying to decide on lunch for the day, be the first to offer an option. Or when you are in a meeting and your boss says, "I want everyone's perspective on this," make a move to speak up first.

As you think about this, notice how you are feeling. Are you dreading this challenge? Are you excited by it? Remember that a lot of actions are avoided because you fear or dread experiencing uncomfortable feelings. Approach this challenge as an experiment and observe yourself when you step out. The goal is taking action and noticing how it feels, not imposing your point of view in every situation. To really maximize the learning from this exercise, remember to measure and reflect. Take a few notes in your journal or on your phone to record your progress.

Identity

Finally, let's notice the challenge to granting permission to feel that comes from your identity. How you perceive yourself directly impacts what you give yourself permission to do. Identity is the meaning you attach to how you show up, relative to a specific group (social identifiers), certain role (doing identifiers), or way of being (being identifiers). For example, "I am single, so I will never be comfortable around married couples," "I am a church member, so I don't lose my temper," "I am an introvert, so

I'm never going to be good at selling my services," or "I'm a math person, so I will be a fantastic tutor for my teen in geometry." I want to draw attention to how your identity specifically challenges your permission to feel. This may seem like semantics, but your words are potent, even when they are unspoken, and your brain is always listening.

When you say, "I am sad," you are identifying as a sad person, versus when you say, "I *feel* sad," you are identifying as a person who is experiencing sadness. If you say you are a sad person, your brain will look for evidence to support your claim—such as lethargy, tears, or loss or increase of appetite. While these are often how you experience the emotion of sadness, when you make it your identity, you lose sight of the things you learned earlier about emotions. Whereas, if you say to yourself, "I feel sad," you will still experience the same expressions of the emotion, but your brain can categorize the experiences as a *feeling*, not an *identity*. And feelings are vibrations, neither good nor bad, that deliver valuable information. They are temporary, and you can experience more than one of them about the same circumstance.

This phenomenon is evident with more comfortable emotions as well. What about "I am joyful," as an identity? Yes, you get that lightness of being that accompanies the feeling of joy, and your brain works to support your chosen identity. It can work for a while, but then something that merits a different emotional response comes along, like the loss of a loved one, and your brain is going to struggle. You may not give yourself permission to experience the uncomfortable emotion of grief to help relieve your brain's energy drain. Then you're back to stuffing your emotions into that pit I mentioned earlier. If you say to yourself, "I feel joyful," you still experience all the sensations and physiological responses of joy, but your brain knows that it is a feeling, and because you now know a few things about emotions, you can look to find the meaning, learn from the experience, and let go of the unrealistic expectation that joy is here to stay always because it is part of who you are.

PREPARE FOR THE CHALLENGE OF IDENTITY

Because you're reading this book, you're already creating awareness about the "I feel" versus the "I am" approach to identity and emotion. But to build on that, pay attention to what you say when you express your feelings and notice how those around you express it. If you catch yourself using the "I am" emotional approach, stop and change to the "I feel" method. After you've done this for a week or so, make a note in your journal about the differences you are experiencing.

We've spent considerable time exploring the challenges that can block your permission to feel. Notice which of these challenges resonated with you and, depending on how you are approaching this work, give yourself time to reflect to expand your awareness of how these are blocking your permission to feel. You may want to stop here and create space for building your skills to overcome these challenges or you may want to move forward and just notice which challenges show up on your journey. Whatever you choose to do at this point, your awareness is piqued and your brain is tuned in to provide evidence of the challenges of blame, self-trust, passivity, and identity. When you spot any of these barriers, give your brain a fist pump and be grateful. You are building awareness, and that is the beginning of all work.

TAKEAWAYS

- There are four **challenges on the journey to giving yourself permission to feel**: blame, self-trust, passivity, and identity.
    - **Blame** is a thought process by which you assign the cause of your feelings to forces outside of yourself. It can trap you in your unwanted feelings and outcomes. As long as your feelings are someone else's fault, you can't change them. What you own, you can alter.

- **Self-trust** is having faith you will show up for yourself with respect and kindness, choosing actions that align with your values and goals. Self-trust is a spectrum that runs from self-trust to self-doubt to self-abandonment. When you show up compassionately for yourself, you build self-trust.

- **Passivity** is the intentional avoidance of taking action. It holds you back from permission when it becomes an unconscious pattern of behavior. It keeps you in your comfort zone, which is always predictable. However, growth happens in unpredictability.

- **Identity** is how you perceive yourself, which directly impacts what you give yourself permission to do and feel. You may resist giving yourself permission to experience emotions that seem at odds with your identity.

3

Feel Better

All right, you're now aware of some of the challenges you face when giving yourself permission and it's time to really start your journey. Think about lacing up your hiking boots and grabbing your pack that you have painstakingly loaded with the tools and supplies you'll need to deal with any obstacles the trek could present. You're at the trailhead, and it's decision time. Will you permit yourself to pursue a balanced partnership with your emotions? If you're just scanning through the book, you may want to mark this page so that you can come back and commit later. If you are ready to commit to this journey right now, it's time to officially give yourself permission to feel.

Fill in the blank, and underline or highlight the following statement. (If you're reading an eBook version and/or if you can't stand to write in your book, copy the following text onto a piece of paper or into the Notes app on your phone.)

> I, _____, authorize and commit myself to feel all of my feelings, understanding that they are a valuable part of my humanity, and I will create the space to learn from them, and then choose which feelings I will act upon.

EMOTIONAL LITERACY

I have a client, whom I'll call Dave, who struggles with crying at times when he does not want to cry. He is most susceptible to tearing up when he unexpectedly has to process something about himself—meaning explain why he is doing something the way he's doing it or express how he feels regarding things he is passionate about. He is particularly frustrated when this happens at work.

As we talked, it became clear that Dave felt at odds with his emotions. Expressing his emotions through tears felt emasculating, and he believed that others judged him as weak when he teared up in public. Because we are coaching and not counseling—he was already working with a therapist—when he shared that he viewed his tears as his lifelong enemy, we worked on how to approach the present-day expressions of this struggle. We tackled this by building his emotional fitness, adjusting his current mindset, and strategizing actions that would create the results he desired.

We embarked first on changing his mindset about associating emotions with weakness, and he committed to giving himself permissions to learn to work with his emotions versus fighting them to avoid what he called "appearing weak." This wasn't easy for him, but we worked with the same strategies I'm sharing here, and Dave began to value the information his emotions were delivering by becoming adept at interpreting their meaning, even if they came with tears. Over time, his tears came less frequently as his frustration with emotion faded, and he used tools to process those emotions in new ways.

Dave is not alone. So many of my clients feel functional but out of balance when dealing with ever-shifting emotions. Often, they express extremes, like no longer feeling or recognizing their emotions, or, like Dave, feeling constantly overwhelmed by them. I have many stories of people reaping the benefits of this work to feel in partnership with their emotions instead of at odds with them. In giving yourself permission to feel, you will be attending to your emotions rather than trying to tune them out. In fact, like a small child who wants attention, your emotions get louder when left unattended.

> I want to take a minute to call out what you're not doing in your emotions work. While your efforts here will support a balanced relationship with emotions to build emotional fitness and create the impactful life you envision, you are not going back to work on healing painful emotions rooted in the past that are keeping you from operating at a functioning level in your daily life. When you are not functional in your current life, you can't get up and meet your responsibilities. If you're struggling with this, I recommend connecting with a therapist. Mental illness is real, and like any other illness, needs to be worked out with a person trained to help.

Because you are permitting and committing to this partnership with your emotions, you need to make sure you are speaking the same language as your emotions. Your first step is to grow your emotional literacy. What do I mean by emotional literacy? Well, literacy basically means reading and writing in a way that shows comprehension or knowledge of a subject. It's learning to speak the language of emotions. I remember traveling in France for the first time, many years after my college French lessons. It was my maiden voyage with the uncomfortable situation of being in a country where I didn't really speak the language. Despite the reputation of the French for being impatient with non-native speakers, most of the people I encountered were helpful as I struggled to interact. Likewise, I hope this work will be helpful and supportive for you as you learn to interact in the language of your emotions.

As you give yourself permission to feel, learning to read your emotions will affirm admittance to an area you often avoided and reduce

> **Curiosity opens you up to learning, whereas assumptions can make you believe you already know it all.**

the anxiety of dealing with the unknown. Wouldn't your parent, or you *as* a parent, be more likely to grant permission when there is clear understanding of what is being asked? Let's face it: Some of us are more comfortable and natural at reading emotions. But this is a skill, and it can be learned. The more you learn to read your own emotions, the more you will become adept at reading those of others. Here is the catch: You must view every step of this work with curiosity. Make no assumptions, write no stories, cast no judgments, impose no expectations on yourself or others. Curiosity opens you up to learning, whereas assumptions can make you believe you already know it all.

READING YOUR EMOTIONS

When you are experiencing an emotion, your limbic system is engaged, especially if this is an intense emotion that triggers your survival responses. Intense emotions left unattended lead to intense reactions. Remember, your goal is not to react to every emotion but to experience those emotions, interpret the message, and respond in a way that aligns with your values and vision. When you start observing your emotions, you are letting the limbic system know that it can stand down and bring your pre-frontal cortex into the conversation. In this way, you are not denying or distracting yourself from uncomfortable emotions. You are instead setting yourself up to learn from and manage them.

Ready to get started? Your goal is to learn to identify emotions and how they show up in your body. Studies have shown that people who develop emotional literacy feel less reactive to intense emotions and more resilient in the face of challenges that come with failure and success. Even anxiety due to phobias is mitigated with the development of emotional literacy.

First, you need to get as specific as you can when you observe your feelings. Often, emotions are discussed in broad strokes. As you develop emotional literacy, you want to get more precise. Think about learning a new language: At first, you learn the common, everyday phrases: "Hello, my name is," "How are you?" "Where are the bathrooms?" and "Check, please." But the more you practice and increase your vocabulary, the more you can communicate and recognize deeper meaning in conversations. In other words, you become more literate in that language. In these pages, you are becoming more literate in the language of your own emotions as you increase your emotional vocabulary.

A powerful tool to help you build emotional vocabulary is the **Feelings Wheel**. Coaches and therapists have created many iterations of and many applications for a Feelings Wheel, but the originator is Dr. Gloria Cox in 1982. For our purposes, the Feelings Wheel is a resource to expand your ability to articulate your emotions with specificity. If you start at the center, you'll see broad categories of emotions, but as you move out on the wheel, you'll notice that the broad emotions are broken into more specific labels.

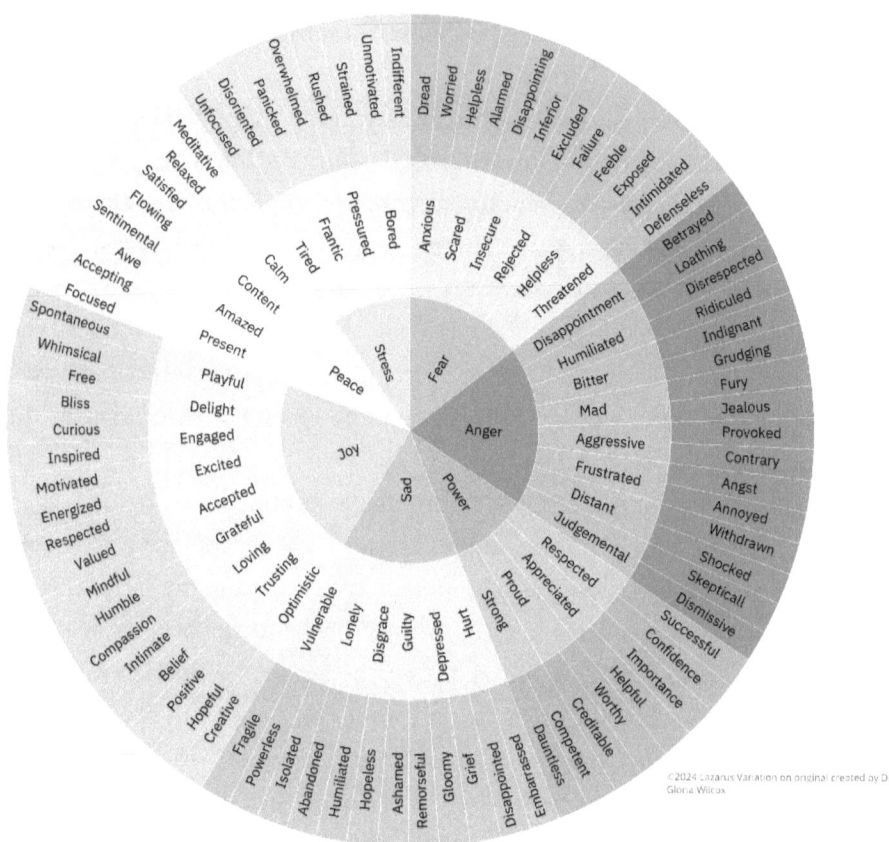

Image 3.1: Feelings Wheel

When you identify an emotion, find it on the wheel. What is that emotion's broad and more specific label? What other labels in the vicinity might be a better fit than the one you initially identified?

Another approach is to take one feeling expressed on the wheel and, as you ruminate on that word, notice if you register a physiological change—a tightening of your chest or tingle along your spine. If you don't, move on to another word, and repeat the process. If you do identify a physical sensation with that word, take a minute to observe what images and stories come to mind. Write down your observations.

Continue this for several days to a week or even a month until you have worked through the wheel. In this way, not only can you increase your emotional literacy, but also studies show that writing about strong emotions for as little as ten minutes can build your emotional resilience.

After you have built your emotional vocabulary with the Feelings Wheel, take it to the next level. Set an alarm on your phone to check in with yourself three times a day. When the alarm goes off, open your phone notes or your journal and record the answers to the following questions. If you'd like support in creating a tracker, here is an example version, or you can download the Emotional Literacy Tracker using the QR code on the table of tools at the front of the book.

EMOTIONAL LITERACY

DAY/TIME	EMOTION	PHYSICAL EXPERIENCE

Ask yourself, "What am I feeling right now?" And the language here is important. You are not stressed; you are *feeling* stressed. Your whole sense of self is not wrapped up in an emotion, but an emotion is a temporary experience that has shown up to deliver a message and enrich your life.

Then ask yourself: "Where in my body do I feel it? What am I thinking that is supporting this feeling?"

So, for example, I might check in with myself at 8 a.m. I'm feeling stressed. I notice this shows up in my shoulder muscles tightening, and my jaw is clenched. My thought supporting the feeling is, "I don't have time to drop off my daughter's tennis racket that she forgot to take to school and still make it to my appointment on time." Then perhaps I check in again at 12 p.m. I feel joy. I notice that with a sort of electric sparkle in my eyes and warmth in my chest. My thought that supports this emotion is how much I enjoyed my morning of work. I love my job.

You're not trying to capture every emotion you experience in the day, just what you're feeling in the moment when the alarm sounds. That's it. The trickiest part is to stay out of judgment. As I shared my examples, you may have had a few thoughts about my parenting or my work, negative or positive. That is judgment. Judgment shuts down curiosity. If you notice self-judgment about the emotions you are recording, don't self-condemn. Instead, say, "I'm just observing here. Isn't that interesting? Look at me being human." Remember, emotions are valuable—no emotions, no humanity.

Besides judgment, there is one other obstacle that a few of my clients have raised. As I said earlier, some of them are convinced that they do not feel. For one reason or another, these clients have learned to tune out of their emotions to survive. Something they've experienced incited them to disconnect from feeling, and it worked, to a certain degree, to get them through a difficult or traumatic situation. I assure them that they do feel, and that they've just stopped noticing. This work helps them notice again. If the situation that provoked a numbing mechanism is a deep wound that needs healing, I help them find a good therapist. When the healing has begun, they can return to building their emotional literacy.

Do this practice for a week. If you find it really challenging or you are not as consistent about it as you would like, go for another week. When you're done, pat yourself on the back for sticking with it, and then look over the data you've collected. What did you notice? What kinds of patterns showed up? What changed over the week as you recorded your emotions?

LIBRARY OF EMOTIONS

Hey, well done observing your emotions, and bonus points if you invested intention and energy in the last exercise. To take this to the next level, you are going to practice choosing specific emotions and putting them on. You'll do this repeatedly and use a variety of emotions to create a Library of Emotions. This will provide you with a reference section of information when you need to understand emotions—your own or others'. When you need a certain emotion, you can borrow it from your library. Ease your way into this, and I'll show you what I mean. We're going from observation to application with an activator exercise, something I refer to as "evocation."

I stumbled onto a rudimentary form of activation when I was very young. When I was in the third grade, I remember being quite pleased with myself and boasting to my friends that I could make myself cry whenever I wanted. I'm not sure why this pleased me, but I did go on to become quite active in drama productions. I did this by revisiting a situation in my young life that made me very sad, but not overwhelmingly sad because a couple of years had passed since the incident. The memory that could evoke a strong physiological response was the experience of my dog being killed by another dog. It could always make me tear up. Again, I don't know why crying on demand felt like an accomplishment in the third grade and, honestly, this memory didn't pop up for me until I started writing this book. Anyhow, that's a little like what you'll be doing—but I promise, no pets will be harmed for the process. You're going to learn to lean into a desired emotion.

To start, choose a photo, a physical photograph or one on your phone, of someone or something you treasure. When you think of the subject of this photo, you get a warm feeling. Now spend some time staring at the photo and recalling the people or subject involved. Maybe you have good memories of when the photo was taken or of the last time you were with that particular person. Now think about how much you love that person, place, or pet. Notice the physiological sensations as you experience your love for the photo's subject. Congratulations, you just activated love, by remembering how you experience the feeling of love.

What did you learn about how you physically experience the feeling of love? For me, my eyes get a little tingly and damp. My chest feels warm and open. The tension in my shoulders relaxes. Choose the physical sensation descriptors that you experience as love and let the photo help support those feelings. This may not be easy at first but keep practicing until it becomes a little easier and you can do it without the photo. I recommend not moving on to the next step until this step becomes easier, where even thinking about looking at the photo generates the physiological sensations.

Assuming that you are feeling confident about the photo exercise, make a quick list of the emotions you observed during your week. As you generate your list, begin filling in your Library of Emotions. State the emotion, how you physically experience it, a memory that evokes that feeling for you, and if you want, a person you think of embodying that feeling—this could be a real person or a made-up representative of that emotion. For example, hopeful Harriet, joyful Jack, the happy elf, the sad puppy, or the discouraged donkey. One caveat if you choose to list an example: Refrain from using anything that has a positive or negative connotation. Remember, emotions are neither good nor bad, and if you want an example to embody that emotion, they should be neither all hero nor all villain.

Notice the emotions that showed up most often throughout the week. Choose one of those to activate or put on next. This could be either a comfortable emotion or an uncomfortable emotion. If this is difficult, start with comfortable ones and work your way to the uncomfortable ones. Please note that working to generate sensations for uncomfortable emotions could trigger some challenging memories. If you feel overwhelmed by these memories, unpack those triggers with a trusted therapist. If you only want to focus on putting on "positivity," you may resist working with building awareness of uncomfortable emotions. But humans are created to feel all emotions—not act on them, but feel them. And to feel them, you must be able to identify them.

Read your description of your chosen emotion and put on those physical sensations. If you need to, recall a situation in your week that engendered those feelings. Caution: We're not judging ourselves! Stay in compassionate curiosity as you build your emotional reference section. We're not rehashing how you should have acted or what you should have said. Just focus on the emotions and the physical experience of the emotions.

Keep working your way through your list. Once the list is completed, create a new list of emotions you really enjoy and aspire to experience more frequently—ones that are not already in your library. The Feelings Wheel may give you a few ideas here. Now note how you physically experience the emotions on your new list. If they are not ones you regularly experience, you may have to use a little imagination to envision yourself in situations where these emotions might arise. Be sure to check out the Emotions Thesaurus in the back of the book (appendix 1) to support this work. A quick word about the Emotions Thesaurus—while not exhaustive, each emotion on the Feelings Wheel is listed. You will find a definition and what that emotion might feel like in your body. (Each of us experiences feelings a little differently, so you decide how accurate the description is for you.) The final entry under each word is body language that might accompany this emotion. If you are struggling to envision an emotion, give the body language under that feeling a try. Adjust your body to take on the postural changes that someone might exhibit when experiencing that feeling. Notice how it feels from that physical space. Fun sidenote—remember how I mentioned that identifying and understanding your own emotions helps you identify and understand other feelings as well? Using this physical mirroring of another person's posture can help you understand what emotions they are expressing.

For a final exercise, I'd like you to check out a specific emotion for a whole day. If that feels like too much, work up to it. Borrow a specific emotion for an hour. Maybe over the timespan of a meeting, or the first part of your day before lunch. For whatever time period you choose, pick an emotion you would like to wear, like choosing a power outfit or just the right sport shoe to feel confident for the big game.

Once you have completed this exercise, you will have made great progress toward not only recognizing your emotions when they show up but actually calling them forward at your will. This is your library, and you just got your card. Now it's time to use it. You can fill in the following Library of Emotions table, draw your own version in your journal, or download a blank template through the QR code on the table of tools at the front of the book.

LIBRARY OF EMOTIONS

EMOTION	PHYSICAL EXPERIENCE	ANCHORING MEMORY

Well done! Notice how much work you have done approaching feelings, building emotional literacy so that you can get an accurate read of the emotions that are showing up, and building the muscle to adjust your emotions to serve you as you take action to move toward your goals. I encourage you to pace yourself with the work you are doing. Skimming the book creates awareness, and that may be all you need for the time being. This sort of soft approach may be all the capacity you have in this season of life. Stay out of self-judgment, and thank yourself for taking the time to do this work at whatever level you can right now. When you're ready, move on, but don't worry, we'll be taking the new skills and tools you've acquired with us. We'll need them for the road ahead.

TAKEAWAYS

- In giving yourself permission to feel, you will be **attending to your emotions versus trying to tune them out**. Like a small child who wants attention, emotions get louder when left unattended.
- **Emotional literacy** means learning to read your emotions. The more you learn to read your own emotions, the more you will be able to read those of others.
- **Your goal is not to react to every emotion** but to experience them, interpret the message, and respond in a way that aligns with your values and vision.
- The **Feelings Wheel**, originated by Dr. Gloria Cox in 1982, is a powerful tool to build emotional vocabulary.
- Tracking your emotions throughout the day can **build emotional literacy**. Be careful **not to engage in judgment about your emotions**, which shuts down curiosity.
- Making note of your emotions will provide you with a reference section of information for when you need to understand emotions—your own or others'. This is called a **Library of Emotions**.
- Remembering **how you physically experience emotions** can help you "put on" or activate them for yourself.

4

Your Superpower of Mixed Emotions

Do you ever have days when you feel like you need to be crazy strong in order to take on every task on your list? What if you had super speed so that you could make those cross-town back-to-back meetings? How handy would it be to leap small buildings in a single bound during rush hour? Before the days of Marvel-movie saturation, a sleeper film in 2005 called *Sky High* tapped into the longing for superpowers. In the movie, the son of two superheroes goes to high school where, to his dismay, because he hasn't shown any signs of inheriting his parent's powers, he is relegated to be a sidekick for other "supers."

No spoilers here, but I want to let you know that you actually do possess superpowers, and you are not the sidekick but the hero of your own story. What superpower, you ask? You are gifted with the superpower of experiencing more than one emotion about the same circumstance. If that doesn't feel like a superpower, look at it a bit closer. Possessing this superpower means that you can experience all the feelings in a circumstance, identify and learn from all the feelings, and then choose which of those feelings will support the way you want to show up. That ability to choose from a full Library of Emotions is a skill that will allow you to create the impact you want, move toward your goals, and fulfill your vision. And that is a superpower.

Give yourself permission. Notice that permission isn't just about giving yourself the authority but creating the opportunity to exercise that authority and learn how to leverage your superpower. At this point, you've done some intentional work of developing feelings literacy. If you haven't and you're just reading ahead, that's okay. Go ahead and get the whole picture before you start applying this stuff. No judgment here.

But if you have been working along as you read, you have developed some emotional muscle for climbing higher, so now let's get a good look at the mountain. Don't stress. It looks big, however, with practice you can not only scale it, you can learn to scale it with speed.

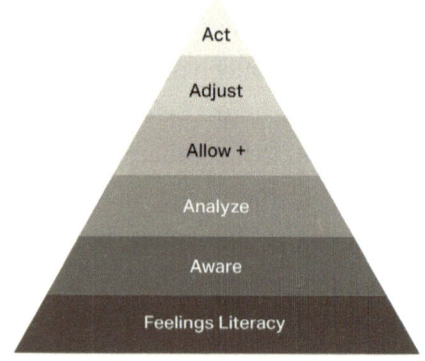

Image 4.1: Feelings Power Pyramid

Like many true mountain climbers before us, we'll start at the bottom. You are now so good at identifying your emotions that you have a solid foundation of emotional literacy. It may seem like you've already mastered identifying, but actually, you've mastered observing emotions in contexts where you may or may not have had any stress around those emotions. Because emotions often come with stress, we're going to learn to exercise the power pause.

The power pause is the time between the inciting incident and the actions (this includes speaking words) you feel compelled to take because of the inciting incident. The power pause is one of the most effective tools because while you have given yourself permission to *feel* all of your feelings, you are not permitting yourself to *act* on every feeling. Be forewarned: The power pause will be longer when you first begin to practice and will shorten, in most circumstances, over time. During each power pause, you climb a mountain.

Because you have become so fluent in your physical experience of an emotion, you may notice the emotion or even the physical experience of the emotion before you accurately notice the inciting incident. For example, you may think, "I'm anxious," and then identify the physical symptoms of your shoulders tightening. Or you may first realize your shoulders are tight and identify that you are feeling anxious before you even have awareness about what has caused you to feel this way. Or, before you identify the feeling or the sensation, the anxiety-inciting incident may be the first thing on your radar. Think about this scenario: You overslept and are rushing to get to work when you discover that someone has parked behind you so close that you can't pull out. You realize you will be late for work, and then you notice your anxiety or your tight shoulders. Whatever order this happens in for you, when you notice the emotion or experience the incident or thought, label that emotion. Give it a name. This tells your brain that it is not an unidentified threat; it's just an emotion delivering a message that you've experienced and survived before. Name it.

You can say, "I'm feeling really anxious." Simple, but not always easy. Stay out of judgment by observing ("There I go, being human again. It's normal.") and understanding ("Well, I'm supposed to feel every feeling, so this is my time to be sad. It may not be fun, but I'm okay with that. I get to be human, so I get to be sad from time to time.") or believing—"If I'm never sad, then I'm never fully alive." Again, this is uncomfortable, but it is normal, human, and temporary.

Now, some emotions appropriately hang around longer than others.

The allowing needs to recognize and accommodate the appropriate timeline to fit the circumstance. The time to allow anger because someone cut you off in traffic is significantly shorter than the time it takes to deal with grief over the loss of a loved one. One brief side note: This discussion is about everyday emotions. There is a real thing called clinical depression that requires specific support. If you believe that clinical depression is what you are experiencing, get help from a qualified therapist and your doctor. And if you're not sure if it's clinical depression or normal sadness, they will help you figure that out as well. Don't ignore it any more than you would cancer or a raging fever.

DOING THE WORK OF ALLOW PLUS

I know this allowing sounds really simple, but it can be super uncomfortable, even painful, and humans can be pretty clever at trying to avoid pain and discomfort. So clever, in fact, that sometimes you don't even notice. One trick is distraction. I call this the Scarlett O'Hara emotional approach: "I'm not going to think about that today. I'll think about it tomorrow." This approach employs busyness to distract from dealing with uncomfortable emotions.

Another approach is numbing undesirable feelings. This can be done with comforts like food, binging *The Great British Baking Show*, or sometimes by exercise or drinking. Each of these things is not bad in moderation, but when numbing happens, they are almost always carried out in excess. Both approaches can be effective for staving off emotion.

Distracting and numbing can be so effective that in an effort to shut out negative emotions, you indiscriminately shut out the positive ones as well. In this way, you can become desensitized to all emotions. They are still there, but you no longer acknowledge them, and you miss the fully alive experience. To effectively experience a rich, human life, you must allow them—not condemn them, squash them, deny them, drown them out with busyness, or numb yourself with other comforts.

A big part of allowing is recognizing and appreciating the message that comes with the emotion.

By now you are getting really good at recognizing by continuing the work of building feelings literacy, but let's pause here to talk about the concept of *allow plus* as it pertains to this segment of your mountain climb. As I'm writing, I am currently experiencing anger and frustration. These words are being produced to the beat of a helicopter thrumming from what sounds like right outside my office window. The powers that be have erected a seventy-five-foot solid steel tower (think smokestack) in the median of my suburban neighborhood street, and a helicopter is passing materials off every ten minutes to workers on the top of that tower. While the noise is distracting, the feelings that I notice, as I said, are anger and frustration. My and my neighbors' views of the beautiful mesa behind our homes are eclipsed by this ugly industrial tower. My home is a mid-70s fixer-upper that is still a work-in-progress, but we saved for ten years to live close to the mesa and have now resided here for twenty-two years.

Why is this relevant to our discussion of the allow plus step? To process these emotions—which I will be doing every time I look out a window or drive down my street—I have to allow that I feel angry, and I need to remember the message that anger brings. The message is not to destroy the tower, the message is that I value my home and why I live here is important. Aesthetics are a high value for me, and I do what is within my control to create aesthetics that are pleasing to myself, my family, and my guests.

My anger is also a driver to take action, but when I can appreciate the information the emotion is providing, I can choose to take action that aligns with my values and purpose. The actions I have taken consist of rallying the neighborhood and petitioning the county commissioners to hear our points of view. This is what I can control. Will it change the fact that there is a huge steel tower between me and my view of the mesa? This is unclear, but I have learned more about how much I value the aesthetics of my environment, which will continue to inform my decisions going forward.

Allow plus helps you sense the purpose of uncomfortable emotions before you take actions you might later regret. Discerning the messages your emotions deliver creates space to choose a wise course. That space is often the difference between making a difference and making a mess. A pioneering idea in psychology often attributed to Viktor Frankl says "Between stimulus and response there is a space. In that space is our power to choose our response. In our response lies our growth and our freedom."

Giving yourself permission to feel is not the same as giving yourself license to act on every emotion. In fact, giving yourself permission to feel creates space. In that space, you understand a few other superpowers: the power to appreciate the richness of being human, the power to make choices that build up others, and the power to keep moving forward.

How are you doing on the climb? Remember, you can pause at any level, and you will still be increasing your feelings fitness. If you're ready to move on, go! The next level in your mountain is *adjust*. You know what you're feeling, it has a label, you've allowed it to be present without self-condemnation, you've discerned the message your emotions are delivering, you've correctly assigned your part in creating the circumstance and the parts that are out of your control, and now you can move further up the mountain and adjust your emotions to serve you better. I know this metaphor of a cute mountain and breaking the climb into steps is a simplification. But simple does not equal easy. Remember to give yourself grace in this process. This is work!

HOW TO ADJUST

Let's look at the tool that helps make the adjust step possible. This template is based on cognitive behavioral theory which holds that cognitions lead to behavioral change. In other words, what you think ultimately determines your actions. Picture your template like this **FETBO Template:**

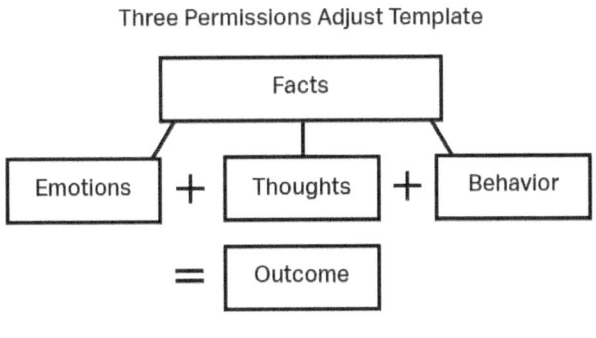

Three Permissions Adjust Template

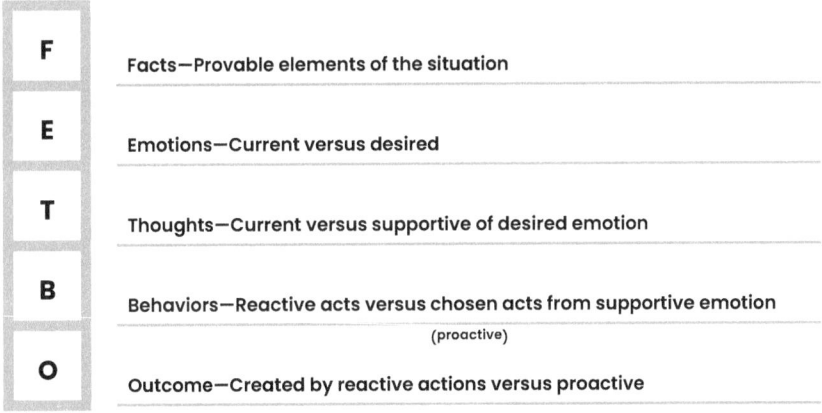

Image 4.2: FETBO Template

F	Facts—Provable elements of the situation
E	Emotions—Current versus desired
T	Thoughts—Current versus supportive of desired emotion
B	Behaviors—Reactive acts versus chosen acts from supportive emotion (proactive)
O	Outcome—Created by reactive actions versus proactive

This could be one of those moments on your journey where you set up camp for a while. The FETBO Template may look complex, but you have laid the groundwork for using this tool. Remember the movie *The Karate Kid* (the O.G. one with Mr. Miyagi)? The karate master built up his student Daniel's muscles by painting, waxing, and boat balancing so that when Daniel began the actual karate moves, he was well equipped. Daniel was amazed at how much he had learned and how much muscle he had acquired without even recognizing how it all fit together. I hope this is one of those moments for you as you summit this mountain.

Using the FETBO Template is not hard; you fill in the blanks. As you focus on adjusting emotions, you are going to fill out two versions of the template. First, a current version—and like Daniel, you actually know a lot of those answers already. A delightful aspect of the FETBO Template is that you can start with whatever blank is easiest. You can draw your own version of the FETBO Template in your journal, or you can download a blank template through the QR code on the table of tools at the front of the book.

Start with your current emotion, using the tower example I shared from my own life first.

F	Facts—I can see the tower.
E	Emotions—Anger, frustration
T	Thoughts—My view has been destroyed. Who gave them the right to bring that ugly thing into my neighborhood?
B	Behaviors—Go yell at the workers blocking my street and building the tower. Rally the neighbors to block in the work trucks with our cars.
O	Outcome—Alienate myself from my neighbors if they don't agree. Make the workers mad and potentially violent. Get my car towed.

Okay, now you have a snapshot of where I am currently. Since we're in the adjust phase, I've already done the work of allowing. Plus, I understand and appreciate the message my emotions showed up to deliver. Now let's adjust and fill out the FETBO Template with the desired emotions and outcomes.

F	Facts—I can see the tower.
E	Emotion—Empowered
T	Thoughts—My objection is legitimate. I can voice my opinion in ways that might make a difference with this tower or could at least make a difference to someone else before towers like this become a standard in my county.
B	Behaviors—Query the neighborhood Facebook group to see if my neighbors share my opinion of the tower. Based on that feedback, reach out to the neighborhood association and county commissioners to understand how this tower was permitted. Petition the energy company about their responsibilities to their customers.
O	Outcomes—Taking strategic actions that align with my values gives me energy. My neighbors and I are communicating and uniting. The power company or county commissioners might be dissuaded from defacing other neighborhoods.

Not bad, right? I want you to notice that once you have filled out your template, you can check your adjustment by noticing if the outcome supports the desired emotion you have written in the E line of your model. To be clear, working through this template is not always a one-and-done strategy. Keep your completed template in front of you until you have followed up with your chosen behaviors. You may even make adjustments to those behaviors as you move forward. Additionally, you may find that other, less desirable emotions may arise about the same circumstance. Work through the steps again to process those emotions.

Congratulations! With your FETBO Template complete, you can summit and take action based on your work. I hear you: At first, you are saying, "Wow, that's so cool. I can actually do this!" Then as you reflect, you think, "Wow, that was a lot of work and took a quite a bit of time. How can I actually do that every time I want to feel all my feelings?" The answer is *practice*. Do this template enough times and you won't need to actually write it out to master the mountain—at least not every time. Even after you have practiced this process many times, you will run into experiences and emotions for which you still need to write it out to work it through. This practice of writing things out creates what psychologists call metacognition, which basically means thinking about your thinking. In your case, you are thinking about your feelings—meta-emotion. So, yes, this is cool, and you can really do this. You will get more adept and faster each time you practice and, yes, sometimes you will still need to create space to write it out and think about your feelings.

GET SOME PRACTICE!

Let's return to the parking example I shared earlier. How would you like to feel in this moment when your car is blocked and you need to get to work? Say you've labeled your emotions as anxious and angry. You've allowed it. "Yep, I'm human, I need to get to work on time, and I am ticked." You've attributed your circumstance in part to yourself for not exercising more care when you parked (noticing what you control and can learn from) and in part to the person who thoughtlessly parked right on your bumper (noticing what you don't control and can let go). Remember that holding on to anger at the actions of others (which you don't control) hurts you, not them. And don't even get me started on the mental impairment, not to mention collateral damage, that plotting revenge can cause.

Now, work the allow plus step by noticing the message your feelings are delivering. Your anxiety could be telling you that you care about showing up to work on time because you value your boss's thoughts about your consistency and reliability. Maybe you care about a promotion that might come your way with your boss's good impression of you. Maybe your anger about the other driver's carelessness is reminding you that you value otherness—the idea that as humans we should be thoughtful about the way our choices impact others. Let your emotions create or affirm self-awareness about your values, goals, and priorities.

Before you work through the adjusting process using the FETBO Template, identify your desired emotion. A word of caution: You don't want to just pull any emotion out of a hat; be strategic in choosing what you will adjust to. What emotions do you want to experience in dealing with the facts of the parking situation? For myself, I would want to move to feeling competent. Setting the desired emotion may sound a little superficial, but it is effective as long as you adjust to an emotion that is believable, applicable, and serves you in this situation. If I decided I wanted to go from angry to giddy with joy, how would that help? Not only would giddiness not serve me, but it would also create a difficult cognitive adjustment—because emotions and thoughts support each other. It would be a massive and illogical jump that would create cognitive and emotional dissonance, which my brain would strongly resist.

Again, ask yourself: What emotions will serve me to get through this situation? For my example, that means adjusting from angry to competent. Here's where your emotional literacy practice supports you. You will want to remind your brain what the desired emotion feels like to help coach yourself through the FETBO Template. Remember how competence feels. When you feel competent, how do you experience it? Where do you carry it? In what kind of position do you hold your competent shoulders? For me, competence shows up as shoulders back and ready for action, chin up, eyes alert, breath activated, and heartbeat slow and steady. Notice each element of that experience and adjust your body to experience the physical aspects of your desired emotion.

Now take a minute and picture a time when you felt competent. One of those "nailed it" moments when you made a great plan and executed exactly. This is where you rely on and sometimes add to your Library of Emotions. Well done! You may have to repeat this step multiple times. It holds easier with practice. You have set yourself up to work through the FETBO Template to determine behaviors that will create the outcome you want. Remember, the template will get easier and more automatic the more you practice.

Finally, you move to the peak of the mountain and *act*. You've already formulated an action in the FETBO Template. You can go straight to the action that you formulated earlier or formulate a couple of additional options now that you have adjusted your emotions and thoughts. I realize this sounds a bit clunky, and honestly, when I read through it, I had a flashback to trying to learn a new board game that had great reviews but confusing instructions. Hang in there—this works. You're at the point in your journey that puts all your feeling skills together. If any part is unclear to you, go back and review those steps again. You will get this and then you'll be amazed at how quickly you process these steps.

The more quickly you put actions to your desired emotions, the easier the transition. It may sound like a quick route up the mountain, or it may feel clunky and time-consuming when it is all laid out. Each step takes practice. At first, don't try to apply this process to every circumstance. Perhaps practice it or even just part of it once a day before you work up to the full process. However you work through it, each step can produce results on its own, so please recognize each step you perform as growth. You can take all the time you need—every circumstance may not require a full summit. Sometimes, it's enough to assess your current emotions and give them names. Sometimes, it is enough just to allow the current emotion without judgment or rash action attached to it. Other times, it is enough just to exercise the power pause and think about your feelings and thoughts.

As you build your emotional fitness, you will be surprised at how quickly you scale the mountain, and you will develop the deftness to just pull out the FETBO Template to work through challenging situations. Your growing emotional fitness will increase not only your processing speed but also your agility so that your occasions of emotional overwhelm or feeling out of touch with your emotions will become more rare. However, similar to your physical fitness resolutions that you practice faithfully until the end of January and then hope that will carry you through a healthier new year, your level of emotional fitness development will be determined by the consistency of your practice.

Since I've been practicing this for quite a while and teaching it to my clients, applying the whole process has become easier for me. But I still work on it, and sometimes it is harder than others. As I mentioned, I don't want to paint the picture that this is a one-and-done lesson. This is a practice, a muscle, that requires constant work to maintain and utilize. You absolutely can do the work, and once you get a taste of the support this work gives, you will be highly motivated to do it.

TAKEAWAYS

- Giving yourself permission isn't just about giving yourself the authority but **creating the opportunity to exercise that authority.**
- A **power pause** is the time between the inciting incident and the actions (including speaking) you feel compelled to take in response.
- You may notice the emotion or even the **physical experience of the emotion** you feel before you accurately notice the inciting incident.
- Recognizing and naming the emotion you feel—without judgment—allows you to remember **it's not a threat; it's just an emotion delivering a message.**
- The concept of **allow plus** helps you sense the purpose of uncomfortable emotions before you take actions you might later regret.
- The **FETBO Template** is a tool to help you adjust to the emotion you choose to feel and act on in a given circumstance in a way that keeps you aligned with your values and purpose.
- **Setting a desired emotion** and putting it on by remembering how it feels allows you to choose to adjust to whatever emotion will best serve you and your goals.

5

Practicing the Permission to Feel

One time, after a skilled pianist I knew mentioned he'd started playing piano at the age of four, I remarked how much self-discipline he must have had to practice as a child. His response was, "My mother was disciplined about *making* me practice." Well, I can tell you after raising three kids and starting them on piano at early ages, the child who made the most progress was the one who practiced because they enjoyed it. I was *not* disciplined about making them practice. I reminded them but didn't force it. When it comes to your emotional fitness, I can confidently say you already have some internal motivation to practice, or you wouldn't have made it this far in the book.

Look once again at the principles of permission—approach, adjust, and act. Here is your English lesson for today: Notice these are all verbs, whereas "permission" is a noun. I'm borrowing this idea from teacher Beth Moore, who says that sometimes we have to "verb our way to our nouns."[1] This means reading the book and even practicing the skills and activities in it once will not be enough to maintain emotional fitness. These things will create awareness and give you an emotional and mental workout, but the muscle comes from practice, and practice comes from motivation.

I have had many clients over the years who want to make changes badly enough that they pay me to help them, but they don't do the work they set out for themselves to do, and as a result, their progress is painfully slow. On the other hand, I have had many clients who come into coaching and practice their action steps so much between coaching sessions that they build awareness and progress toward their goals much faster than I anticipate and I'm working hard to keep up with them. You may say that you forget or are just not a motivated person. Don't worry—I'm not scolding you about practice; I sincerely want you to go at your chosen pace. But I also want you to be aware that your progress is determined by the pace you set for yourself. Let me introduce you to an activity to help you tap into some motivation to practice.

One of the most powerful skills you can develop in giving yourself permission is to know how to motivate yourself to actually *act* on that permission. I know this is work. Remember: You can just work on a segment of permission to feel and still make a difference in your feelings fitness. But to build your current motivation, let's borrow that motivation from your future self.

Use your paper journal or Notes app for this exercise. Answer this prompt: What would it look like if you could skillfully learn from and leverage your emotions instead of feeling at the mercy of them—at home, in relationships, at school, at work? Really explore each area of this question. How would life be different? Grab hold of that vision.

Now ask yourself: What would the result be if you continue as you are? Would you feel at odds with your emotions or lack of emotions? Would your relationships be growing? Would you be aligned with your values and achieving your goals?

Write it out. It doesn't have to be poetry, just a few bullet points that state what the effects of permission to feel could create, and same for the effects of not doing the work. Maybe post these reminders as your phone lock screen or tape this journal page to the bathroom mirror to keep them in front of you as you work on these exercises and practice climbing the mountain. This is why you're doing the work. When motivation lags, look at this list and create space for the emotions that accompany both visions. Those emotions will help motivate you to practice, whether it's to help you connect with the feelings of remaining the same or creating new ways to thrive.

GET YOUR BEARINGS

I know you may be reading the book before you actually jump into the work. As I've said before, even that will yield powerful results of creating awareness and setting a strong foundation for the slower-paced process of building your permission muscles. Whatever your method, now is a good time to see where you are in the journey. Let's look once again at your Permission to Feel Map.

Image 1.1: Permission to Feel Map

When you first looked at the map, you knew you were at the beginning of this journey. Now, I want you to find where you are on your own permission to feel journey. Take the quick assessment that follows to find your growth edges for this trip. Growth edges are areas where you want to build more muscle to keep moving forward toward feelings fitness. Rate how strongly you agree with each statement on a scale of 1–10, with 1 being "I strongly disagree" and 10 being "I strongly agree."

> **Assess**
>
> To what degree do you agree or disagree with the following statements?
>
> —— I understand and embrace the principle that I am created to experience but not act on all emotions.
>
> —— I recognize that emotions are not good or bad but instead are vibrations in my body that deliver important messages to expand my self-awareness.
>
> —— I can catch myself blaming others for my circumstances and emotions.
>
> —— I rarely use the blame response.
>
> —— I trust myself to recognize and follow through on changes that are good for me, align with my values, and move me toward my goals.
>
> —— I can recognize when passive tendencies show up in my thoughts, words, and actions.
>
> —— I am rarely passive in expressing my opinion, making decisions, and taking actions.
>
> —— I know my values; am clear on my strengths, weaknesses, and goals; and feel confident about who I am in the world.
>
> —— I can recognize and specifically label my emotions and how they show up in my body.
>
> —— I can allow uncomfortable and comfortable emotions and accurately interpret the messages they deliver.
>
> —— I can use the FETBO Template to adeptly adjust my emotions to create the results I want.
>
> —— I can choose actions that respond to circumstances and align with my values.

Notice the areas that are not a 10 on your assessment. What could you do to bump them up one number? This will help you set goals to keep moving toward feelings fitness. Choose one element of your assessment that you want to work on as a specific goal. To select this element, look at the statements for which you gave yourself a lower number. The more specific you are, the more successful you will be at measuring your progress and the more accurately you can adjust if you are not progressing toward your goal. (Tip: Be sure to set alarms and calendar reminders to support working on this goal.)

BUILD A REFLECTION HABIT

While I'm not suggesting you live in the past, rest on your laurels, or weary your arms patting yourself on the back, taking a few minutes to remember past instances when you felt rushes of desirable feelings can produce powerful motivation. I know we just assessed where you are on your journey, but now we are talking about a practice of reflection—not just where you are but how you are. Think of moments when you experienced things like joy or relief, received or gave gratitude or help, and set a goal and achieved it. These reflections help you get a more accurate look at the circumstances and people in your life that incite desirable feelings, how aligning with your values stirs strong emotions, and what lessons you can take away from your past experiences. A recent Harvard study explored the benefits of reflection for professional development. The researchers found that there is a direct correlation between the success of leaders and their reflection habits. In the study, a pattern emerged about the most beneficial content of those reflections.[2] We'll talk more about this in the next section, but for now, let's check your position.

No matter where you are after your evaluation, honor the progress you are making by noticing and measuring as you practice. Remember, measurement matters, and it can be just a quick check-in at the end of the day, some notes taken on your phone or in a journal. Here are some questions that can help guide your reflections:

- What went well in your feeling journey?
- Did you keep your emotions log?
- What is the biggest challenge to identifying your feelings?
- Did you label your emotions today?
- How effectively did you allow an uncomfortable feeling without it driving unwanted words or actions?
- Were you able to analyze accurately the people, events, and thoughts that sparked that emotion?
- How often did you focus on what you control?
- What did you notice about adjusting an emotion that wasn't serving you well?
- Did you choose an emotion from your library that served you better?
- What kind of actions came out of your chosen emotion?

I'm not saying you have to answer all these questions every night. Just pick one or two and rate yourself on a scale of 1-10, or just capture your response in a few words. Start noticing the moments—big or small—when these steps are helping. Write them down with a date. When you review your journal, you'll be able to not only measure your progress but to notice how you are in the process.

Also, keep practicing. Set new goals as you progress. You are looking to build emotional muscle. While your map may show that you've arrived at "Feelings Fitness," as with any form of fitness, you must stay active to maintain your levels. Think of goals not as a destination but as mile markers or trail guideposts that build your confidence to keep going. You gave yourself permission to take this journey. No matter what element of this work has your attention, you are building awareness that will improve your relationship with your emotions.

Now that you have created a reflection experience, I invite you to make it a habit by establishing a reflection routine. Because we're talking about feelings and motivation, I encourage you to connect with this task of building a reflection habit by contemplating meaningful moments in your lives that arouse desirable emotions.

You can support this reflection by collecting reminders of past moments that created feelings of victory. In other words, keep a victory file. This can be a physical file, or you can build the file on your computer or phone. This file can include journal entries that document your journey through a particular challenge that pushed you to overcome obstacles or threats and create the results you wanted, or just moments when you recorded gratitude about something or someone wonderful in your life. It can include artifacts of success, such as a canceled check or bank statement, a press release, a letter congratulating you on a promotion, or a thank-you note from someone you impacted; essentially, pieces that signify a goal achieved. Also, you can regularly add to your file as you continue your journey.

The real benefit is not in creating the file so much as building a habit of spending some time connecting with your feelings about the file contents and thinking about what you can learn from the patterns that emerge. As you sit with your file in whatever form it takes, continue to support reflection by asking yourself a few questions: What feelings are stirred when you review your file? How are you experiencing them? What values are showing up in this collection? What percentage of your time and energy is going toward creating similar experiences in your current schedule? What does this file say about how you're showing up in the world? What would you like to pursue to add to this file? Once again, we're going for building a new routine of reflection. Set an appointed time each week to spend in reflection. Treat it like any other appointment: Put it in your calendar, set a reminder, and guard that time. We'll be adding other elements of reflection later in your journey, but you can get started building this habit and reaping the benefits right away.

I want to again encourage you at this point in your journey. You have created awareness, added skills, and are building new strength to support emotional fitness. You may be experiencing a bit of fatigue, but it is my hope that you are also feeling a sense of accomplishment. This is not an easy path. Just as if you are on a challenging hike, you start feeling sore and stiff from the unfamiliar work of navigating new terrain. Bear in mind that you can rest, pace yourself, and notice how far you've come. We're not going for instant mastery but progress. If you are flagging on this journey, consider getting some extra support, someone who may want to work on their own feelings fitness or a coach to partner with you as you travel. However you go and at whatever pace you choose, you can give yourself permission to approach, adjust, and act your way into your own version of feelings fitness.

TAKEAWAYS

- **The principles of permission—approach, adjust, and act—are all verbs.** Sometimes, we have to verb our way to our nouns.

- Your motivation will drive how much you practice, and **practice is what will improve your emotional fitness.**

- **Reflection helps you gain clarity** about the people and circumstances that evoke positive emotions, how aligning with your values fuels those feelings, and the lessons you can learn from past experiences.

PART II

Permission to Fail

Mission Mindset: Failure is **for** you.

// "Failure is not an option." That is a line from the movie *Apollo 13*, often attributed to the character of Gene Krantz. In reality, Mr. Krantz never said that. However, he is quoted as having said in an interview, "When bad things happened, we just calmly laid out all the options, and failure was not one of them. We never panicked, and we never gave up on finding a solution."[1] When you examine the full quote from Mr. Krantz, it may be more accurate to say that "giving up was not an option." However, "failure is not an option" makes a great sound bite, especially considering the stakes in that situation—human lives. In fact, it was failure that put the crew of Apollo 13 in peril in the first place. What you miss by embracing the catchy line "failure is not an option" is noticing that only after many failures in practicing the solutions did NASA come up with one that would succeed. In the movie, there is a scene where they need a new oxygen filter for the LAM. They dump out all the parts and keep trying to fit something together, failing until they don't. There is another scene in which the character of Ken Mattingly is in the simulator trying to figure out the power sequence for reentry. He keeps failing until he doesn't. Again, this situation had the high stakes of human lives.

Unfortunately, somewhere in your survivalist brain, you tell yourself that every failure has the stake of human life—specifically your life. It is not true and, believe me, NASA had plenty of lower-stakes failures. In fact, much of NASA's success was derived from creating environments to practice and fail with low stakes before they moved to gradually higher-stake attempts.

Most failures in your daily life do not result in death for yourself or others. Yet you can develop the idea that all failure is the ultimate negative instead of simply an approach that didn't work to learn from and try again. What if you could boldly step into actions that move you toward your vision of an authentic and impactful life without dragging the heavy weight of a paralyzing fear of failure?

In Part II, you'll learn how to build a new mindset regarding failure, including uncovering the challenges of failing, identifying ways to fail more effectively, and practicing how to leverage critical thinking to learn from your failures. In this work, you must give yourself permission to approach failure, make adjustments to your thinking, and take actions that will not eliminate failure but reduce fruitless failure. While it sounds simple, you will need all your emotional fitness to do this work.

6

Planning to Fail: Failing Map

While discussing feelings in Part I, I touched on thoughts, particularly regarding mindset. Now that you are feeling in partnership with both comfortable and uncomfortable emotions, let's go a bit deeper into mindset and turn greater attention to the role that your thoughts play in how you show up in the world. You are moving into new terrain but taking with you the lessons learned earlier on the trail. I want to share what the map for the second part of your travels looks like.

Image 6.1: Permission to Fail Map

FAILING PERMISSION SLIP

Just as before, let's see what it takes to give ourselves permission to fail. In Charles Dickens's *A Christmas Carol,* Scrooge sees and hears the ghostly chains his deceased business partner, Marley, is dragging around. He asks Marley about it and Marley answers, "I wear the chain I forged in life I made it link by link, and yard by yard; I girded it on of my own free-will, and of my own free-will I wore it. Is its pattern strange to *you*? . . . Or would you know, the weight and length of the strong coil you bear yourself? It was full as heavy and as long as this, seven Christmas Eves ago. You have labored on it since. It is a ponderous chain!"[1]

The chain I'm asking you to look at is not crafted from selfish acts or miserly ways; it is forged of uncomfortable emotions from failures past that you choose to feed, ruminate on, allow to master you, and even become a part of your identity. It is forged from forbidding partnership with your emotions and prevents you from failing well. Failing well means learning and leveraging your failure lessons, even sharing them so others can learn, instead of adding a heavy link that you try to hide as you drag it along in your daily life. When Scrooge asks Marley to comfort him regarding the "ponderous" chain, Marley had no comfort to offer, but I do. Be comforted, dear reader—you can lose this chain and use its lessons to be of good to yourself and others.

How do you lose the chain? Instead of telling yourself that failure is not an option, adjust your mindset to treating failure as part of the process. That sounds simple, but it will be a bigger leap for some than others—yet a bigger leap is doable for anyone when it can be broken down into small steps. First, let's give ourselves permission to create an environment with gradually higher stakes to build up failure tolerance. And you can use the Permission to Feel Map to process uncomfortable emotions that arise. Together, we'll see what happens when we accept that failure is not only an option but also a vital step that supports your pursuit of growth and impact. Permission to fail creates freedom, humility, learning, and ultimately success.

I once had a client I'll call Jane, who came to her session with me seeming a bit lower in energy than usual. She was taking a step back into higher education by enrolling in an entry-level college course. As we talked, it came up that she struggled with confidence about passing the class. We continued to discuss different elements she felt were holding her back. She had a supportive spouse and employer, and she genuinely wanted to achieve a higher level of education. She felt motivated, had done solid classwork, received excellent grades, and had good attendance. So why was she so deflated about her chances of passing the class?

With her willingness to be vulnerable in our conversation, Jane was able to notice that an experience of failing a major exam she'd taken in her early twenties was determining her mindset about her current chances of success. Jane's failure had been traumatic to her, as the exam had been part of her corporate training, and it had drastically altered her career path. Since then, Jane had always been very intentional about avoiding thoughts or conversations about this past failure. I asked Jane what emotions were coming forward when she thought about possibly not passing this class. She mentioned shame, sadness, and self-loathing. I learned that since that failure, she had gone on to have several work promotions, a joyful marriage, and three healthy children. I challenged Jane to notice the value in that failure.

After thinking a bit, she began to speak softly. "Well, I got a wake-up call about time management—so I took my next training for a new department seriously. I actually learned a lot about self-discipline. Now that I think about it, I have a lot of empathy and patience with those I train for my team. I don't want them to keep failing."

Next, I asked Jane what she would tell her twenty-one-year-old self who had just failed. I could see that she was struggling with the emotion of that question as her compassion for her younger self showed up. She said, "It's going to be okay. Everything works out for the best."

Based on what she said in our session, I challenged Jane to notice how valuable the lessons of that failure were to her current self. She came back the next week and shared that she had been able to talk to a young team member who had failed at work and actually shared her failure story. "I have avoided talking or thinking about that time ever since I was twenty-one, but I can now see it as a foundation to empathize and encourage others. It is actually a valuable part of my story." The uncomfortable emotions Jane experienced when thinking about that failure were eclipsed by the desirable emotions of compassion, warmth, and fulfillment. Remember: Most failure is not fatal but instead is fertilizer for growth.

Let's take another look at how performance is affected by permission to fail. In tennis, when you start feeling like things aren't working with your game, you can get tentative, and the first thing to go is probably your footwork. But the second thing is that you can get cautious and shorten your follow-through swing. One of my daughter's tennis coaches so perfectly exemplified the power of permission to fail that it is forever etched in my mind.

One time, during a particularly tough match, my daughter and her tennis partner were struggling to even get points on the board. Their coach called them over between games and told them, "I don't care if you win another point or not, but you move your feet and take a full swing with follow-through every time." The girls still had to play challenging opponents, but they no longer needed to focus on how they were failing. The players had permission from their coach to play and fail. They didn't have permission to quit.

You can probably guess what happened. They played in freedom. Their feet started moving more freely, and the hits had full follow-through. They came back and won the match. I also witnessed that coach say the same thing to other players; his words had the same effect even if they didn't bring the same results. The players didn't always win, but they felt so much better walking off the court knowing they moved and played with freedom and greater confidence because they had their coach's blessing to try and fail.

What is it about having the freedom to fail that helps you succeed? It doesn't guarantee success, but it does remove the mental pressure that curtails innovation, creativity, and confidence. Some would say that freedom takes more than permission, and I'm not denying that skill and practice are involved, but when it comes to execution, permission to fail is crucial to the experience. With permission to fail, learning isn't short-circuited by shame. You can bolster your courage that failure is not only a possibility but also a stepping stone for your ultimate goals. Hear that again: Failure is a stepping stone. It is not a stopping place.

> **Failure is a stepping stone, not a stopping place.**

I'm not sure where I picked up this metaphor, but I like the image: What if after leaving your house to go to work or the grocery story, you were almost there and suddenly you had to stop for a red light? What if you took that to mean you could go no further, and you turned around and went home? Or even worse, what if you took a red-light encounter as an identity and said, "Well, I guess I am not a green-light kind of driver," and parked your car permanently? In any case, you would never get anywhere.

If you treat failure like a red light that says, "Go no further," you will not accomplish the impactful things you want to do. I'm not saying that failure is fun or comfortable, but it builds your strength to keep moving forward. Think about the way you build muscle. You have to lift enough weight that it stresses your current muscle. You have to work to muscle failure. If you don't, you never give the muscle enough stress to tear and create new muscle, and you also don't discover your current limits so you can strategize how to surpass them or work around them. Most of us never even get close.

Brené Brown states that the courage to be seen and vulnerable comes before confidence.[2] I agree, and that confidence is created by embracing the possibility of failure and knowing that you will survive, learn, and eventually thrive from it. So how do you have enough courage to give yourself permission to fail?

THE PERMISSION MINDSET

If you haven't already picked up on it, permission is a mindset. A mindset is basically the way you repeatedly think about things. That is a simplified definition, but it gives you a foundation. The permission I am talking about says:

- I can do this work.
- I can grow through this work.
- I can build my emotional fitness.
- I can develop skills to handle failure and learn from it.
- I can learn to fly to heights of success beyond my first thoughts.
- I can use tools to create an impact that benefits myself and others.

This is a permission mindset. It's the belief that you are not tied to your current skills, wiring, or circumstances and you can create strategies to keep developing. Read that last sentence again. I hope you can feel an opening up to the possibility of permission.

Carol Dweck in her work *Mindset: The New Psychology of Success* calls this a growth mindset: "In this mindset, the hand you're dealt is just the starting point for development. This growth mindset is based on the belief that your basic qualities are things you can cultivate through your efforts." Dweck attributes thoughts that hold us back to a different thinking habit that many of us have developed, which she calls the "fixed mindset." She defines the fixed mindset as the repeated belief that you will die the way you were born and cannot improve your lot. It says that you are born with a certain amount of intelligence or talent, which cannot be changed or improved upon.[3] To fully give yourself permission, you must have a growth mindset.

> **Mindset is a thinking habit.**

At first, you may say, "I have given myself permission, and I have no problem with a growth mindset." Maybe you are right, but let's have a little closer look at how your mindsets show up. Think about your language choices: "I get to" versus "I have to," "I want to" versus "I should," "I choose" versus "I can't," "That's impossible" versus "Let's look at other options." Look at how a fixed mindset might show up in your identity: "I am not a math person," "I am a perfectionist," "I'm so disorganized," "I'm always late," "I'm just one of those people meant to be single," "I'm not center stage material," "I'm not made for C-suite," or "I'm not artistic." Notice the resignation and internalization of these labels, and please recognize the power of mindset.

Remember, a mindset is a thinking habit based on your beliefs. It's not just a fleeting thought. Your thinking habits are embedded in deep neural pathways. You can change them, but it will take consistent intention and focus. So, when you catch a thinking habit that supports a fixed mindset, be kind to yourself but gently say, "Ah, there is that fixed mindset. I know, brain, you're trying to protect me but I'm giving myself permission to change this habit." Check out the next section for greater mindset awareness.

Getting into the Permission to Fail Mindset

Practice adopting the following beliefs to shift into a permission to fail mindset.

Awareness over acceptance: A permission mindset is one that acknowledges embarrassment, shame, guilt, despair, anxiety, defeat, denial, disgust, jealousy, loneliness, unease, worry, and overwhelm. While this is not an exhaustive list, it is enough for you to notice that these bring varying degrees of discomfort. Remember that you are not trying to avoid these emotions. It is okay and normal to experience uncomfortable emotions. They show you that you care, remind you of what you value, and draw attention to the gaps in your approaches. Your work here is to expect and allow these uncomfortable feelings to do their job, thank them, and then let them go. You do not set up house with these emotions, but instead do the work to shift your focus and feed emotions that help create the results you desire. If you don't feel in partnership with your emotions when it comes to failure, spend more time on the exercises in Part I of this book. Notice the "do not enter" signals that your brain sends out but do not accept them as inaccessible or unchangeable. Call it out. Let's say you hear yourself say, "I'm just not a motivated person. I think that's a fixed mindset. I refuse to accept that I have to stay feeling unmotivated."

Compassion over criticism: Once you call it out, your brain may try to protect you with an old defensive thinking habit. (e.g., "You've always been unmotivated, you're born that way, you're following in your parents' path—they never finished anything. You're just like them.") Replace that with compassion. (e.g., "It's okay to feel unmotivated. In fact, it's growth that I recognize it, and I can improve my motivation with specific tools and strategies.")

Curiosity over judgment: Judgment may say, "Stop thinking anything is going to change," "This is too hard for you," or "You're not good at this kind of work." A permission mindset gives you permission to ask questions. Get curious: "What if I was feeling motivated?" "What would that look like?" or "I wonder what I can do to feel more motivated?"

Training over trying: "But we can try," was a precious phrase integral to my oldest daughter's conversations, mainly when she was about three. Anytime I, in my distracted grown-up way, explained the difficulty, even impossibility, of something she was curious about and wanted to try, she would, in her most hope-filled intonation, end the conversation with: "But we can try." And more often than not, I had to agree with her. "Yes, sweetie, we can try."

"Mommy, what would happen if my cars and I took a bubble bath when we get home?"

"Well, that might be fun, but Mommy needs to make dinner. I don't know how I could cook in the kitchen and sit in the bathroom while you take a bath."

"Mommy, we could order pizza for dinner, so you don't have to cook."

"Well, that's true. We could, but I already put the chicken in the fridge to thaw for tonight's food."

"Mommy, we could cook the chicken tomorrow and eat pizza in the bathtub."

"Yes, we could, but Daddy might be sad if we eat dinner before he gets home."

"Mommy, would Daddy be sad if he missed dessert?"

"I don't think so because Daddy took cookies in his lunch, so he probably won't eat dessert tonight."

"Mommy, we could order pizza so I can eat cookies in the bathtub?"

"Well, I think that might spoil your dinner."

"Mommy, but we could try."

Of course we went home, and she had a bubble bath—and yes, we compromised: She had one cookie in the tub, so she still had room for dinner. Trying is great. It is hopeful. Trying is often touted as an example of grit—get back up on the horse and try again. However, a permission to fail mindset is powered not so much by try, try, and try again, but by treating each failure as training. You are training yourself for success every time you learn from a failure.

By even just going through these beliefs one time, you are starting to change your neural pathways and move toward a growth mindset that supports permission. And these beliefs repeated consistently over time will literally reroute your thinking and change your brain.[4]

POSITS OF PERMISSION TO FAIL

Failure teaches us about ourselves. When you give yourself permission to journey with failure, self-learning is accelerated and deepened, meaning you grow faster and develop deeper roots. Preparing for permission to fail by noticing and planning for potential challenges is part of your approach.

Think about creating a strategy for a long and challenging trip. You prepare and pack the appropriate tools, but you don't know how effectively those strategies work until you start using them in an actual tough trail situation. Circling back to my friend on her Grand Canyon hike, remember she packed enough food for the whole trek because she didn't want to rely on having to purchase food along the way? She also set alarms to remind herself to nourish. She didn't know how hard it would be to make herself eat when the alarm sounded. She knew in her mind that it could be hard, but she learned that despite fatigue and nausea, she had the willpower to follow through on the commitment to eat when her alarm sounded.

Recognizing gaps in your self-knowledge teaches humility, which helps you be open to learning that might otherwise be missed. It is highly valuable to learn you are not bulletproof from the consequences of your actions and the uncomfortable emotions that result from failure. However, you can learn how to handle the wounds and build skills to compensate for the gaps you identify in the process.

Failure provides evidence that you can survive the uncomfortable feelings that accompany failing. Not until you fail and still wake up the next day, whatever that looks like, do you know for certain that survival is really possible. When you reflect on a past failure, you can see and be assured that you can survive future failure. This feeds your confidence, but it also provides the perspective to risk failure in the future and encourage others as they take on risk and fail as well.

Failure can help you separate who you are from what you do. This is a powerful principle that we will explore more later in the book. Similar to the identity work you did in Part I: Permission to Feel, where you noticed that you are not what you feel, your failures provide the opportunity to notice that you are not what you do. Who you are shows up in how you do what you do, but your results don't determine who you are.

Failure gives clarity to the path forward. When you pay attention to the information failure gives about your results, your learning can inform the action adjustments needed to create different results. If you change nothing, nothing changes. You know that if you want to change your results you have to change your actions, and to change your actions you need to address your thoughts and emotions.

> **Failure gives clarity to the path forward.**

Failure streamlines your decision process. Because your decisions rely heavily on what you feel and think, accurately processing the emotions and thoughts that accompany failure can reduce the mental load required for making future decisions. This principle doesn't give us an excuse to stop trying based on past results, but it challenges us to stop putting energy into the same actions, hoping they will create different results—a process Einstein labeled insanity.

Failure builds identity muscle. Experiencing failure while maintaining a strong sense of self builds strong identity anchors, just as adding more resistance increases physical muscles. We'll talk more about failure and identity in a few minutes.

> **Failure builds identity muscle.**

When you review the principles of failure, it seems logical that pursuing failure is a beneficial choice. But should you really set out with a goal to fail? Doesn't that go against all the information about creating neural pathways that serve us? And what about manifesting your vision? Following your dreams?

It is my goal for you to see that you are not pursuing failure, but pursuing action. Permission to fail is about taking action without the paralyzing fear of failure—actions based on clear thinking and strategy that take the possibility of failure into account. You are going to learn to let go of thoughts that keep you in a cycle of failure or thoughts that keep you from taking action because it might result in failure. Permission to fail releases you from focusing your energy on playing to not fail and enables your energy to help you play to improve. But remember, permission is a choice, and the ball is in your court.

CLARIFYING FAILURE

In trying to find a way to approach failure, it can be helpful to take a Failure Inventory. What does failure mean to you? What are some failures that loop in your brain when you reflect on what failure means? Make a list of past failures. These can be specific or general—as long as they are things you have actually experienced. Some examples from my list are:

- Not answering an email from a friend
- Missing a deadline
- A bad grade on a test
- Not finishing a project
- Not sending a thank-you message
- Agreeing to meet but never following up

- Investing in an idea but never creating a return on that investment

These are just a few of mine, but now it's time for you to make your own list. Notice, as you do this, when uncomfortable emotions arise. Remind yourself that this is observation from a place of curiosity and is not intended to judge or shame. When those emotions come, receive their message—you are experiencing them because something about them reveals things you care about. Thank them for showing up and either let them go or let them know you will continue to learn to process them.

To move further into your objective observance, imagine for a moment that you are looking at a stranger's list. Have you ever watched Ramit Sethi's documentary series *How to Get Rich* on Netflix? As part of this show, he looks at the financial statements of strangers and tries to discern information about who they are, their spending habits, and what is important to them. He stays out of judgment. I want you to do this with your failures list. Look at the list as if it is someone else's. What can you tell about this person's failures?

If I do this with my aforementioned list, I notice: This is a person who likes to please others, who is driven to achieve, who may see big vision but struggles with executing the details. Interesting, right? Noticing your failure patterns helps you continue to expand your awareness. Resist slipping into self-judgment.

Now that you have made these observations, what advice would you give to someone whose history contains these failures? Here is my advice to a person with the failure list I generated: First, well done on valuing achievement—you have a drive to achieve and are continuing to push forward toward impact. Relationships are important to you, so take steps to align with that value—this will require time management and admin support. Details are often a struggle for people with vision—surround yourself with people and strategies to help you execute your plans.

Did you notice what is missing from my advice? Identifiers, condemnation, excuses, quitting, and disappointment. My advice to myself gives me permission to fail and learn from it. What advice did you come up with? You don't have to actually take your advice, but observing and advising from an outside viewpoint will help you take perspective of your current permission to fail as it applies to actual failures in your life. It also helps you understand what you consider failure.

I mentioned that you would visit permission challenges in each phase of your work—to be prepared for each leg of the journey. Be careful, challenges can be stumbling blocks or steppingstones.

TAKEAWAYS

- **Failure is a vital step that supports your pursuit of growth** and impact. Permission to fail creates freedom, humility, learning, and ultimately success.

- **Failure is a stepping stone, not a stopping place.**

- Failure is not fun or comfortable, but it **builds your strength to keep moving forward.**

- A **permission mindset** is the belief that you are not tied to your current skills, wiring, or circumstances and you can create strategies to keep developing.

- In trying to find a way to approach failure, it can be helpful to take a **Failure Inventory.** Noticing your failure patterns helps you continue to **expand your awareness.**

- When you reflect on a past failure, you can also be assured that **you can survive future failure**, which feeds your confidence and provides the perspective to risk failure in the future.

7

The Stumbling Blocks of Failure

’m looking at it as I write. It is one of my favorite possessions. It is a masterpiece, not because it was created by a master, but because the meaning it holds is masterful. It is square-shaped, made of off-white clay, with a heart cutout slightly off-center. It has many textures and splashes of blue, purple, and green. The best part is a jagged angular piece broken off from one side and glued to the bottom. This creation was made by my middle daughter when she was three years old. She made it in preschool, and every time I look at it, I feel the joy of her three years of learning and creating. I'm so grateful for the teacher who encouraged my girl to take the broken piece and attach it as a decoration before firing the clay. Of course, the piece reminds me of my daughter, who is now finishing her master's degree, but it also reminds me that the greatest success and learning comes from the ability to see the areas that are broken and leverage them into growth and beauty.

Image 7.1: Creating Beauty with Broken Pieces—Art by Michaela White (Age Three)

Please don't think that I am downplaying the pain of trying and failing. It is not fun, and it's not all roses and sunshine. Also, just like learning to acknowledge and process uncomfortable feelings, in giving yourself permission to feel, sitting and mourning the loss of what you hoped to achieve is important, human, and normal. Camping in that grief, using the experience of failure as an excuse to not try again, or allowing it to be a shortcut in your thinking does not serve you or those around you. Permission to fail is work, and it is uncomfortable and takes energy, but to support that work, let's look at some challenges you can plan for along the way and see how you can make something beautiful—not because you avoid the challenges, but because you work through them. Then your failures can be part of your own masterpiece.

I mentioned at the beginning of the book that you would be looking at the same challenges in each permission. However, the challenges may present differently based on the permission you are traveling through. Returning to our Grand Canyon hiking metaphor, one hiking challenge you must prepare for is choosing the right shoes—not so much for how they look but how they perform, although I do love a cute shoe! As you can imagine, over the course of a Grand Canyon hike you will encounter different terrains. Even though your footwear is the same, its performance will vary based on the terrain you are traversing. Let's examine the challenges you will face in the terrain of failure.

BLAME

How does blame present when encountering failure? First, remember your challenge of blame from Part I. How are you making progress in noticing your blame response? I want to help you get more clarity about your locus of control.

Depending on what obstacles my clients are facing, we often take some time sorting their lives in a way that helps them discern what they can control and what they cannot. I use the idea of three buckets that I introduced at the beginning of the book. This can support your work with the blame response because while we're not assigning blame, you are stewarding your energy. Remember: What you own, you can alter.

Think again of the illustration from the Introduction with the three buckets: things you can control, things you can influence, and other. You can sort most of your existence into these categories. This work helps inventory what you own and can alter if you choose. In your control bucket are your actions, your thoughts, your emotions, your goals, your plans, your dreams. In your influence bucket, consider how you can often influence your relationships, your health, others' plans, others' feelings, others' thoughts, and others' actions. You can sometimes influence community, national culture, or policies. And in the

> **What you own, you can alter.**

other bucket goes anything you cannot control or influence. This is not an exhaustive list but notice that how you steward your energy and attention will determine the contents of each bucket.

As you work to change your habit thinking in the area of blame, look at your part of each bucket. You have 100 percent control of the control bucket, and that will require a lot of energy if you are owning your part, but you only have varying degrees of influence in the middle, influence bucket. Look to invest an appropriate amount of energy first in what you can actually influence. Watch out when you might be tempted to slip into blame in these areas. Blame is not always incorrect, but it is rarely helpful. Expend as little energy as possible on things that fall into the third, other bucket.

But isn't it irresponsible to not call out those who are responsible? Actually, there is a difference between holding people accountable and blaming. Let's look at an example. One freezing winter, my husband and I were in the process of helping my mother-in-law renovate a rental property after a long-time tenant had vacated. The property manager wanted to keep the process moving even more than we did so she could get a renter in as soon as possible. Because of this, she authorized the installation of a newer thermostat. We weren't sure why she did this because the old one was still working. However, my husband and I went to the house to work on the punch list for the contractor estimates and discovered the new thermostat. While it was not the thermostat we would have chosen or in the place we would have chosen to put in, we could adjust. The real issue was that it was not working. The house was freezing. Even though we messaged the property manager about the issue right away and left faucets dripping to prevent the pipes from freezing, she did not fix the issue until the following day. The damage had already been done over the previous few nights, and there were some leaks in the pipes.

When we called her, instead of using a blaming statement like, "You authorized a replacement thermostat without consulting the owner and now you will be paying for the repairs to fix this," our approach was, "What seems fair in this situation? What can we do to avoid this breakdown of communication in the future?" We knew the property manager would be on the defensive if we came in blaming, but that a curious approach would provide an opportunity for us to influence future results. We could not have achieved that result if we'd led with blame. We understood that we could control who was involved by firing the property manager or putting her on the defensive so much that she quit. She had been a good manager up to that point, and we didn't want to drive her off or damage the relationship. We also knew we could not control some of the quirks of the property or the weather. Many elements of that project were in the influence bucket. Instead, we chose to spend our energy on creating clear communication systems, making strategic choices, monitoring the process, and having influential conversations with the others involved.

You've already practiced noticing where blame shows up in your thinking. Now spend some time noticing what you can own or influence and what you cannot and therefore belongs in the other bucket. Then make sure to empower yourself by owning your part and empower others by not leading with blame.

**Where do you want to spend your time, energy, and focus?
It's your choice.**

Image 0.1: Three Bucket Theory

SELF-TRUST

The second stumbling block you want to plan for is self-trust—having the belief that you will do the best you can to show up for yourself with respect and kindness, no matter the result of your efforts, the circumstances, or what anyone else says. You spent some time creating awareness during your first look at self-trust in Part I and worked on cuing a stronger relationship with yourself. Don't miss that self-trust is a relationship. Remember how emotions provide information? The same is true of failures. Both failures and emotions are opportunities to collect data which translates into deeper self-insights. By doing the work in these pages, you are gathering deeper insights into yourself.

That is how relationships with others grow as well. The more time you spend together, the deeper insights you develop about each other. You develop inside jokes and shared memories.

> **Self-trust is a relationship.**

In relationships with ourselves, you build these insights by reflection. Reflection is spending time with yourself and processing memories and insights that come from people and experiences in the outer world. I know we have already discussed building a habit of reflection, but I want to make sure you recognize the benefits of that time to your relationship with yourself. Beyond the work in these pages, are you creating time to reflect? Perhaps your only time for reflection is when your head hits the pillow at night. Unfortunately, this is not always helpful as it can disrupt your sleep. Not because the reflections are uncomfortable—though they often are—but because your brain processes reflection with almost the same intensity as it does an initial experience. The discipline that comes from meditation practices can help us rein in and calm mind chatter at night. Since there are many resources for and approaches to meditation widely available, I'd like to focus on how to build self-trust by creating *time* for reflection. This will have the side benefit of helping reduce your mind-chattering pillow talk.

Remember that the definition of self-trust is the belief that you will do your best to show up for yourself with respect and kindness. When working with clients who have presented a challenging situation for support in a session, I often ask how they want to show up in that situation. Once they have defined how they want to show up, we look for strategies that will set them up for success in showing up in their desired manner. Similarly, you are looking to show up for yourself with respect and kindness. What strategies can you employ to accomplish this goal? You can provide evidence to yourself that you will spend time processing, reflecting, and ideating with kindness and respect.

One way to provide this evidence is to set and keep appointments for that processing, reflecting, and ideating. Often, my clients are leaders in high-pressure positions and have very busy schedules. I sometimes recommend the discipline of meditation to them, but another strategy we use is blocking time in their calendars to spend with themselves. This is similar to the parking lot strategy often employed in business meetings. When a group gets off-topic from the meeting agenda, the leader says, "That topic merits more discussion later. Let's put it in the parking lot for now." Then, they add the topic to a list labeled "parking lot."

For my clients, I recommend they keep a "needs more thought" list. The trick is that if you want this list to build self-trust, you must already have an appointment blocked on your schedule for giving those things more thought. You can label this time "focus thinking" or "notes-to-self time" or even "super thinking," but you must protect that time and keep that appointment with yourself. When you do, you give yourself evidence that you will show up for yourself. I also recommend you do this with journaling, although many of my clients include journaling as a part of their morning or evening rituals. But it's the same principle: Journaling time is protected, and you show up and do it consistently. No relationships thrive when one party consistently stands up the other party—the relationship with yourself included.

PASSIVITY

The third challenge to look at within the perspective of permission to fail is passivity. I want to look at a particular form of passivity: perfectionism. To be clear, perfectionism is not only in the realm of passivity, but it can be an element of it. I realize perfectionism might not be noticeable as passive at first glance, so let's take a deeper look. Let's get clear on how you are defining perfectionism. For us, a simple working definition of perfectionism is looking at life through a lens of unachievably high standards for yourself and/or others.

Now, there is a difference between having high standards or expectations and having *unachievably* high standards and expectations. Perfectionism falls under the passivity stumbling block because it inclines us to all-or-nothing thinking that can paralyze us and is actually a thinking trap that perpetuates a cycle of paralysis. At some point, you use this way of thinking intentionally. Then you begin to use it often enough that you come to rely on it to function and feel better about your results, and then that reliance becomes a habit, so that you hardly notice that you are choosing perfectionism.

Are we all perfectionists? No, but an increasing number of us are. And it can be tricky because you may choose perfectionism in some areas and not in others. For example, you may feel that your work projects must be perfect before you can hand them to your boss to approve, but you feel fine if your home is consistently untidy.

So why is perfectionism increasing? One huge contributor is social media. I don't mean to attribute all the ills of society to social media because I believe it does have great benefit. One downside, though, is the curated images people post as if they were everyday life—beautiful, happy photos that give the impression of living the best life ever. Unfortunately, it's human nature to compare yourself to others. As a result, you may feel your life falls short after only a few minutes of exposure to these curated, sometimes even staged images. Of course, everyone wants to present themselves well, but it's easy to lose sight of the context and contrast of social media versus actual life.

While not an exhaustive study of all the contributors to this increase, in their 2016 study, Thomas Curran and Andrew Hill confirmed that perfectionism is increasing over time. Curran and Hill found that Millennials have higher expectations for themselves in the areas of academics, achievements, careers, and body image. Their study also found that between 1989 and 2016, the self-oriented perfectionism score increased by 10 percent, socially prescribed perfectionism increased by 30 percent, and other-oriented perfectionism increased by 16 percent. Curran states, "Today's young people are competing with each other in order to meet societal pressures to succeed and they feel that perfectionism is necessary in order to feel safe, socially connected, and of worth."[1] That is strong stuff!

Think about your basic needs—security, safety, and connection—all increasingly tied to unachievably high standards. No wonder stress, anxiety, and depression are on the uptick. What's interesting is that the more you hold unrealistic standards of perfection, the more vulnerable you are to burnout, anxiety, and depression, all of which can lead to passive thinking.

We'll explore the emotions tied to failure, but for perfectionists, failure often triggers shame because they fall short of the unattainable standards they set for themselves. This reinforces the belief that failure is unacceptable, leading to avoidance of risks and new challenges. As a result, they become paralyzed, stuck in a cycle where fear of imperfection leads to inaction, which leads to more failure, more shame, and a deeper sense of stagnation. Coming up, your work in the beliefs framework will further enhance supportive mindsets by breaking perfectionist thinking habits.

Just a quick side note: Remember how I talked about the blame habit? Some of us wield perfectionism as a blame shield with no small amount of pride. "Oh, I know I'm being hard to work with, but I'm a perfectionist." Basically, this is telling others to suck it up and get used to your unachievably high standards because that is just the way you are and it works for you. (Anyone noticing the fixed mindset here?)

But does it really work for you? Does it help you try new things? Not procrastinate? Work well with a team? Make decisions easily?

According to Stephen Guise in his book *How to Be an Imperfectionist,* "Perfectionists are driven mad or frozen in place by the chasm between desire and reality, which impairs their ability to progress and enjoy life."[2] The good news is that there are many tools and practices that can help change your perfectionist ways.

I want to make sure you don't leave these pages without creating awareness about how perfectionism may be supporting passivity for you. We've talked about some of the phrases that, when used frequently, point to perfectionism thinking. You may have noticed some of them as speech patterns in your own life. Another characteristic that perfectionists share is the standard of never letting anyone down—ever. Perfectionists use this standard to self-motivate and to avoid uncomfortable emotions like shame and guilt. This makes failure particularly difficult because what you perceive as failure is multiplied if other people are inconvenienced or have to deal with uncomfortable emotions because of you.

This is also passive because when you engage in perfectionist thinking and want to please everyone, you struggle to set and hold boundaries. Those impossible standards to please mean your personal needs, desires, and goals take a back seat to literally everyone else. I struggle with this one myself.

Here is a simple activity I call the VIP Exercise to bring clarity about how much this desire to please is utilizing your energy and focus and who is getting the lion's share of attention. I challenge you to write out a list of all the people whose opinions really matter to you. Just brainstorm the list while thinking about those you have recently worked to please (or not be a bother to). Once you've generated the list, put these individuals in order of importance to you. Really notice how much mental and emotional energy you have spent to please these people and consider whose opinion of you does and doesn't actually impact your life. This exercise is not an excuse to be a jerk; it's designed to create awareness about the impossible standards you cling to and who you are investing energy in trying to impress.

To further expand this awareness, notice how often you desire to impose your impossible standards on those you care about—your spouse, your child, your co-workers, and so on. Awareness is the beginning of all work, my friend. Catching your thinking habit in the area of perfectionism will empower you to break that habit.

IDENTITY

Who do you say you are? This bears repeating: You are not your feelings, and you are not your failures. You are a living, breathing, evolving human who will feel and fail and fly. Remember our definition of identity as the meaning you attach to how you show up relative to a specific group (social identifiers), certain role (doing identifiers), or way of being (being identifiers).

Simplified, identity is how you define yourself. Other than social identifiers, like your ethnic, religious, and gender identities, you likely often define yourself by what you are doing or what role you are filling at that moment. I'm a mom. I'm a CEO. I'm a pilot. I'm a tennis player. I'm a daughter. I'm a spouse. "I am" statements have power as emotional identifiers, though it is possible to shift them, thereby remaining emotionally flexible, without threatening your identity. It's not that doing identifiers are wrong or need to be avoided. In fact, they are a concise way of communicating your current roles. They only become stumbling blocks when you attach too much meaning to them. This is because your roles change frequently, sometimes unexpectedly, and if your identity is only anchored in your role, you experience disorientation that can keep you stuck until you restore your former anchor or replace it with a new one.

An identity that supports a mindset of permission is primarily anchored in your being identifiers so that it cannot be dislodged when those doing identifiers shift. For example, if you identify as *being* creative, your mediums can change but your creativity remains. I am creative, and my medium is drawing. I am creative, and my medium is writing. I am creative, and my medium is food. I am caring, and I care for my children. I am caring, and I care for my clients. I am caring, and I care for those who are experiencing homelessness. I am a hard worker. I work hard to keep my home clean. I work hard to create value for my company. I work hard to manage my finances. I work hard to take care of my parents.

Even when you are skilled at separating your being from your doing, you can still trip when it comes to defining failure and even success, which we'll see in the next permission. When you anchor to doing identifiers and you fail in your doing, you almost automatically label yourself a failure. But you don't have to anchor to *doing* identifiers. To turn this stumbling block into a stepping stone, I challenge you to anchor to *being* identifiers.

The next exercise I'll take you through is one of my favorites because it does the powerful work of making visible some of the invisible concepts that shape your existence as a human. Basically, that is another way of saying it creates awareness. I'm confident that by now we have spent enough time together for you to sense that awareness is a big part of my work, and I hope that when you hear the word "awareness," your brain is automatically completing the thought: *Awareness is the beginning of all work*. But don't be satisfied with staying at the beginning of the work. Don't miss that once you create the awareness, measurable impact comes from *acting* on that awareness. I can look at case studies and learn that failure can be a stepping stone, but until I do the work of believing that it *is* a stepping stone, then testing it by stepping on the stone of failure to learn, and then adjusting and taking more action, I'm not creating outcomes that are any different from when I treated failure as a stumbling block. Do the work of uncovering your identifiers in this exercise and you will be equipping yourself to use failure as a stepping stone to reach your next success.

To determine your being identifiers:

- **Free write:** Set a timer for three minutes. Ask yourself what words describe you and capture every being descriptor that comes to mind. Think along the lines of some we've already talked about: creative, caring, hard worker, and so on.

- **Check your values:** List your top five values. They will point to some of your being identifiers. Let's say your top values are faith, family, kindness, money, and education. Check to see if "I am spiritual," "I am nurturing," "I am a producer," or "I am a learner" fit as identifiers. If so, add them to your free writing list. (If you need help identifying your values, check out the QR code on the table of tools at the front of the book to see the values work I do with my clients.)

- **Reflect:** Look at the following list and see if any other identifiers resonate with you. Remember, these are being identifiers, not aspirations. These descriptors should fit how you already see yourself.

  - Authentic
  - Bold
  - Compassionate
  - Courageous
  - Determined
  - Devoted
  - Empathetic
  - Encouraging
  - Fearless
  - Generous
  - Gracious
  - Hopeful
  - Inclusive
  - Joyful
  - Kind
  - Loving
  - Mindful
  - Nurturing
  - Optimistic
  - Passionate
  - Quick-witted
  - Resilient
  - Supportive
  - Tenacious
  - Understanding

What do you do if your identifiers are all negative? If you can only generate negative identifiers such as, "I am forgetful," "I am slow," or "I am careless," pause and do a few minutes of activator exercises to charge the prefrontal cortex and move from judgment into curiosity. Dig deep into looking at your values and appreciate the identifiers that accompany those values. Often people who identify as forgetful are also innovative or visionary. For some people, details are difficult and they can be perceived as forgetful. A person who values quiet thinking or deep research can sometimes be perceived as slow, as they desire a lot of information and analyzing time before they act. With your values in mind, self-compassion, and active curiosity, look at your negative identifiers and search for powerful identifiers that are their flipside and align with your values. If you're still struggling, reflect on any positive feedback you have received or go to a person who knows you well and whom you trust. Look for words that describe the strengths others see in you. Try on some of those as identifiers.

But aren't "I am" statements supporting a fixed mindset? Actually, you are making anchoring statements. Think about an anchor. It is a tool that keeps a boat grounded, but it can be pulled up so the boat can move and change its location and even its mission. You are choosing these statements, and you can change them as well. Just as an anchor can be moved, so can your being identifiers—if you want to. Some you may never want to change, like "I am kind," while others like "I am a hard worker" you may change to suit the season of life you are experiencing. If you're changing this identifier because you retire or reduce your work hours, you might choose as your anchor instead: "I am devoted," "I devote time to tasks that bring me and others joy," "I devote time to caring for my grandchildren." There is similar energy shared between hard work and devotion, but the motivation has changed. Remember: Being identifiers are a powerful tool to grab on to when your doing identifiers change.

Once you've generated a list of being identifiers that resonate with you, narrow them down to three. You may need to try on a few sets to get the ones that feel fitting. Plug your top three identifiers into this sentence and post it on your bathroom mirror or phone lock screen and say them out loud at least once a day.

"Today, I am _____, _____, and _____."

When you encounter failure or success, make your statement again. This will support your brain in easily accessing these identifiers, regardless of your circumstance.

THE FEELINGS OF FAILURE

Since you are building skills about how to deal with failure on a foundation of permitting yourself to feel, let's not overlook the specific feelings that keep company with failure. Shame is the most overarching feeling, and one you're probably most avoidant of. But remember that emotions are vibrations in your body that are offering you messages. Research shows the feelings that go along with failure are often what you are trying to avoid more than the physical results of that failure.[3]

Since you have given yourself permission to feel, you'd think you would handle feelings of failure pretty well. However, humans are emotional creatures. Those emotions can creep into your blind spot and take you by surprise. Let's take a moment to reflect on what these feelings might look like.

I have a client who, when his mother would come to visit, would be so filled with dread that he couldn't look forward to spending time with her and instead would keep trying to plan things to prove that he was worthy of love to evoke from her a response that fit his expectation of a loving mother's behavior. Somehow, he never felt like he got it right.

He loved his mother but was stuck in this cycle of dread, performance, disappointment, and shame, where he felt like he was failing as a son and she was failing as a mother.

He told me that through his work with a therapist, he realized that at a certain point in his young adulthood, his relationship with his mom appeared different from relationships his friends had with their mothers. His mom wasn't as involved as some of his friends' moms, and she didn't act the way his friends' mothers did when he visited their homes. He worked for years as an adult to create moments for her to step up and be the mom he dreamed of, and when she didn't, he grew sad and angry, which morphed into shame. He brought this issue into our coaching because while his therapist was helping him deal with his hurt and disappointment from his childhood, he felt that his present time with his mother could be improved, and he wanted my support to see what that could look like.

> **The feelings that go along with failure are often what you are trying to avoid more than the physical results of that failure**

While his emotions were understandable, they were not serving him in his present relationship with his mom. He had some thinking habits and beliefs that would need to shift. We examined the messages his current emotions were delivering and worked through the FETBO Template to focus on more supportive emotions and thoughts that could create the results he desired. When we focused on the elements that he could control (spoiler alert: his mother wasn't in his control bucket), things began to change. He realized that he was judging her love for him and how she behaved during their visits based on his expectations—which were based on beliefs about what a "good mother" should be—while completely missing that her expression of love for him could be the visit itself.

He became aware of what he could and could not control and let go of his idea of what a "good mother" should look like. He let go of his own behaviors that were efforts to evoke responses from her. My client examined his beliefs, adjusted his expectations for his mom, and learned to appreciate who she was now without basing her love for him on his expectations. He also noticed his identifiers were constantly threatened because he wanted to identify as a loving son, but he kept experiencing shame and anger when it came to his mom. He clarified what it means to be loving: spending time with and being kind to his mom. He started noticing how often he did those two things and gave himself evidence that he is, indeed, a loving son. It was a process.

Now when his emotions cue him into slipping back to unrealistic expectations (a longtime thinking habit) or self-talk that brands him as unlovable and unloving, he checks his thoughts and makes adjustments as needed. I want to point out that he has to continue to do this work, but it goes faster and more easily the more he does it.

We just walked through a lot of information and practices. How is your journey going? What are you doing to pace yourself and replenish? Remember: This work is for you, and your return on investment of time and energy is exponential, but you also need to be mindful that it is work. Circle back to anything that feels unclear. Talk with a friend and share what you are learning to solidify your takeaways and get their perspective. Nourish by noticing how much you have already accomplished. Celebrate your efforts.

You now have a lot of awareness and hopefully are feeling some muscle starting to form to aid you in giving yourself permission to fail. Understanding how to recognize and manage these stumbling blocks will support you in failing well.

TAKEAWAYS

- You will face **four challenges in the terrain of failure**: blame, self-trust, passivity, and identity.

  - **Blame** diverts your energy away from gathering all of the essential information that failure provides. In the wake of failure, blaming others for their actions is a less effective use of time and energy than healthy accountability practices.

  - **Self-trust** is a relationship you must work to build with yourself. Engaging in self-reflection after failure is an opportunity to collect data, which translates into a deeper understanding of how you want to show up in your life.

  - **Passivity** often manifests as perfectionism: the habit of holding standards too high to achieve. For perfectionist thinkers, failure begets shame for not living up to their impossible standards. This reinforces the disempowering notion that failure is the fault of their perfectionism, rather than a direct result of their efforts.

  - **Identity** is how you define yourself—a mix of being and doing identifiers. These ideas about who you are can hold you back from giving yourself permission to fail if you do not cultivate flexibility. By anchoring your identity to those *being* identifiers, you can maintain your sense of self even if your *doing* identifiers shift and change to reflect your newfound permission to fail.

- **Shame** is the most common feeling associated with failure. But remember that emotions are vibrations in your body that are offering you messages. You can use that information to take the action that best serves you.

8

Fail Better

In the fall of 1991, eight scientists chose to be sealed for two years into a biosphere in the Arizona desert. Their goals were education, eco-technology development, and support for NASA in developing life support for long-term space missions. The biosphere covered three acres and is to this day the largest closed system ever constructed. While it contained many species of plants, the trees that grew within the biosphere were of special importance. The scientists noted that the trees in the biosphere grew more rapidly than they do in the outside world. But despite their rapid growth, these trees would collapse before they reached their full height. As the biosphere occupants struggled to understand the reason for this, they discovered that the trees lacked deep roots and their wood did not harden to the expected level. That is when they realized what was missing for these trees to flourish: strong wind.

In nature, strong wind over time encourages tree roots to grow deeply to help stabilize the tree. The other response to the bending and movement of a tree when it encounters strong wind is something called stress wood. This wood is much harder than the wood found in the biosphere trees. In much the same way, our human failures cause us to build resilience because of the presence of uncomfortable emotions. If you never encounter emotions that are challenging to process, you never have the chance to develop deep roots of wisdom and strong skin of emotional and mental management. Failure is a strong breeze that, instead of avoiding, you can learn to leverage. When you learn to fail better, you can reach the full height of your potential and grow strong in the face of resistance.

FAILURE LOOP: ENTREPRENEURS, SCIENTISTS, AND TERRORISTS, OH MY!

Only recently have researchers turned a bright spotlight on failure. One such researcher, Dashun Wang, associate professor at Northwestern's Kellogg School of Management and director of the Center for Science Innovation, sought to understand what determines those who ultimately succeed or fail beyond just trying and trying again. You may have guessed from the heading of this section that Wang and his colleagues chose three disparate groups to study when looking for patterns that would reveal how to calculate failure and success: entrepreneurs, scientists, and terrorists.

Wang and company wanted to be clear on what success and failure looked like for each group. For entrepreneurs, success was determined by the amount of venture funding they received. For scientists, success was based on how their grant applications were rated. And for terrorists, success was defined by how many people were wounded in their attacks. That last criterion feels a bit gruesome to call "success," but each group was evaluated on its success in achieving its *stated objectives*. These are certainly three very different groups for comparison.[1] The study revealed that success cannot be predicted based solely on how often and how hard you try, but instead on how well you learn from the previous attempt—in other words, how you leverage learning from failure. Those who analyze the different components of their failure and look for feedback from others significantly impacted the success of their next attempts.

One article about Wang's study says, "The very worst learners incorporate zero information from their previous tries, starting from scratch on every component every time."[2] Wang himself stated that those with a low chance of success "thrash around for new versions . . . wasting valuable time going back to the drawing board again and again."[3] This sounds a lot like the principles of permission: **Approach** the failure by looking at what worked and didn't work and getting feedback, make **adjust**ments to the components that didn't work, and take **act**ion by trying again.

I went to a workshop a few years ago where different helping professionals presented about their work. The first presentation was by a cuddlist. You read that correctly: cuddlist, or a helping professional who cuddles their clients. She works with people who are touch-deprived. As she described her methodology, she asked the workshop attendees to participate in an exercise she does with every new client. She told us that no matter what she asked, she wanted us to tell her no. She went around to each participant and asked if she could hug her or touch her hand or touch her head. The first few people she asked felt a bit awkward but by the time she had reached the last participant, we all had experienced a powerful practice in saying no.

Just as the crowd's awkwardness at saying no reduced, I want the uncomfortable feelings that accompany your failures to reduce as well. You can learn to fail better by increasing your tolerance for failure while practicing compassionate self-talk. When the discomfort that accompanies failure arises, notice it with compassion and curiosity. Continue to process the uncomfortable emotions as discussed in Part I: Permission to Feel.

To this end, I would like you to challenge yourself to try one thing every day at which you will probably fail. Pick something low stakes, something as simple as asking for a discount at a restaurant, shooting a snowball from your front door into your neighbor's basketball hoop, picking up a new dance step, trying to park perfectly straight, baking a cake if you've never tried that, juggling, balancing a book on your head, signing your name with your non-dominant hand, and so on. Choose small things. The outcome doesn't matter—just get used to challenging yourself. As you take on these challenges, remember to speak to yourself kindly throughout the whole process. Speak as if someone you dearly love was trying to accomplish the task and you want to offer them encouragement. Think of an endearment or a nickname that captures how you want to show up. You can use a doing identifier as this endearment, even if you don't comfortably embrace that title, as long as you don't say it to yourself with sarcasm. An example might be "Okay, writer, let's tackle that next chapter." This part may be more difficult for you than the initial task. Get used to encouraging yourself through the challenge. Laugh and stay out of judgment.

After your tolerance for challenge and the potential for failure has increased, choose tasks with increased stakes. Challenge a stronger tennis player to a match, take on a challenging school or work assignment, or write an article and ask for feedback. For a quick win with your self-talk, simply shift your internal conversations to the third person and imagine that the third person is one of your best friends or loved ones. "This is impossible. I don't know how I'm going to get this all done in time" can instead become "Okay, this is tough. But, you'll get through it. You'll get done what needs to be done." Studies have shown that even that small shift helps you activate your prefrontal cortex, regulate your emotions and thoughts, and choose your next steps with more objectivity.

I encourage you to journal about this experience. Just quickly jot down the date and ask yourself how you failed today, how you felt about it, and what you said to yourself. Here's an example of the beginning of a journal entry: "I failed at parallel parking today, which made me feel annoyed and stupid. I said to myself 'I suck at this,' and drove on." After some failure practice, an entry might look something more like this: "I failed at parallel parking today. It made me proud, and I told myself, 'Way to go for trying something you find difficult,' but I also felt a little embarrassed as I pulled back out into traffic and drove on."

Now that you've begun to practice failing, you may have noticed other areas you categorize as failure. Maybe you've always observed them. Maybe you can't stop noticing them. If you haven't already, it is time to transfer that of kind self-talk from the practice failures to the real-life failures. So next time you miss a work deadline, your teacher says you're not applying yourself, you apply for a dream position but don't even get an interview, or you submit your work and promptly receive a rejection letter, be kind, get curious, learn, adjust, and try again.

You are doing great. How do you know? Check your journal. At this point, you have increased your tolerance for failure and learned how to speak kindly to yourself as you pursue failure. Sounds good, right? Actually, even though I hope you have practiced each of these steps, mastery is an unrealistic expectation. You know that those unrealistic expectations leave us vulnerable to perfectionism, so let's instead form really clear, achievable expectations. We've all spent years developing our old ways of dealing with feelings, failure, and flying. Some of us are just tweaking our methodology with the exercises in this book, while others are going for radical adjustment. Either way, this is a process by which you measure progress, not mastery. Just as it has taken years to get where you are, this process takes time. Circle back or camp out on the exercises that you find challenging. Also, anticipate life handing you experiences that will require more effort to process how you feel about them. Life presents us with many opportunities to practice this work.

I want to show up authentically to you, and I want you to know that you are not alone in this work, so here is what my own practice looks like. Because I teach people how to do this and I'm supposed to be "the expert," it's easy for me to regress out of self-compassion and into self-criticism when I notice my own patterns of excuses and blame. It's when these thinking habits show up that my inner critic can take over my self-talk. I feel ridiculous when I realize it, and I feel shame. The ugly self-talk that plays on repeat in my head goes something like this: "If you can't use these tools and practices to help yourself, then who are you to speak to others, you self-righteous hypocrite? You deserve to be sick and disabled." It can get mean, and it can be so stealthy and subtle that it becomes pervasive before I even recognize it. But oh, is that inner critic in trouble once I do.

Practicing journal reflection helps me catch on faster, and with that awareness, I can then replace my "I can't because . . ." mindset with an "I can try because I'm stronger than I think" mindset. Or I can apply a "breathe and train" mentality to the situation. These are my truths: I know I'm stronger than I think and as long as I have breath, I will give my best effort. I also add my endearment to make sure I am not chastising but encouraging myself. I say these things to myself aloud. There is something about speaking a statement out loud that makes it more real, as both my inner and outer selves hear it. If I find myself slipping into judgment, I use the curiosity and activator exercise to get myself back on the truth track.

CHECK YOUR FAILURE MINDSET

Let's conduct a quick mindset check. In this work to process failure, I have talked with you about the challenges. You have systematically worked to build failure tolerance. Additionally, you've seen an example from nature that illustrates the supportive role that failure plays in development. You have also seen some scientific reasons as to why failure is not only necessary but helpful for success. With all of this new information, increased awareness, and work on failure tolerance, how is your mindset regarding failure?

Remember that a mindset is a collection of beliefs and attitudes you hold about yourself, your life, and the world around you. Check in with yourself to see if you are developing more of a growth mindset regarding failure or if you're feeling resistant to this work because of a fixed mindset about failure. Mindset determines the effectiveness of your efforts and the impact of the results you will create. A growth mindset regarding failure says:

- "I can fail better."
- "I can learn from failure."
- "I can use failure as a stepping stone."
- "Failure makes me stronger."

But a fixed mindset about failure says:

- "I am a failure."
- "This work cannot change how failure affects me."
- "I can't recover from failure."
- "Failure is just my lot in life."

If you are still finding yourself entrenched in a fixed mindset regarding failure, reacquaint yourself with the mindset work in the introductory sections of this book. If you feel that is not the kind of support you need, or you don't want to take the time to do that right now, read on. When you notice the language of a fixed mindset internally or externally, try to simply address it with curiosity. Ask yourself, "What if I didn't believe that?" You don't have to answer that question, but just asking it may loosen the grip that fixed thinking has on you.

TAKEAWAYS

- Emotions that are challenging to process help **grow deep roots of wisdom and emotional and mental management.** Learning to leverage failure will help you reach the full height of your potential and resilience.

- Experiencing failure in low-stakes situations will **increase your tolerance for challenge and the potential to leverage failure.** When the discomfort that accompanies failure emerges, notice it with compassion and curiosity.
- **When failure arises, practice compassionate self-talk.** Start during your low-stakes failure practice and then transfer your compassionate self-talk from practice failures to real-life ones. Be kind, get curious, learn, adjust, and try again.
- Check in with yourself to see if you are developing more of a **growth mindset toward failure.** Mindset determines the effectiveness of your efforts and the impact of the results you will create.

9

Leveraging the Lessons of Failure

Our brains are sense-making machines. That being said, brains don't always latch onto lessons that serve us and help us move forward. To ensure that your learning is put to good use, you have to intentionally funnel your brainpower to learn helpful strategies and inform the evolution of your permissions.

Our next tool will help you focus your brainpower to look at past failures and make sure you are creating valuable takeaways. Studies have shown that your brain has trouble discerning between actual experiences and experiences you are thinking about. This is why you get similar physiological responses to seeing a car accident in a movie and being in a car accident in real life. Note, however, that I said *similar* not *identical*. Actual experiences are combined with physical sensations that produce stronger impressions than simulated experiences.

Why does this matter? Remember that you are giving yourself permission to fail, whereas your more natural inclination is to avoid failure at almost any cost. Remember that your brain wants you to remember your failures because it codes them as threats, and it wants you to be very aware of threats that should be avoided. Notice how you are working instead to **approach** failure to learn. You have worked to overcome that natural inclination by discerning how to process uncomfortable emotions and desensitizing yourself to some of the discomfort of failure. It's important to understand that you are giving yourself permission to approach and not avoid. You are intentionally approaching a circumstance that you may have invested a lot of time and energy into avoiding. In doing so, you will learn valuable lessons and lighten your mental, emotional, and even physical load.

Notice, in the work of these *three permissions*—to feel, to fail, and to fly—I want you to learn from the past and apply that learning going forward, but this is not the work of looking to heal a past wound. Sometimes, as a byproduct of coaching work, your reflection on past failures uncovers a wound that is not healed. If this is the case for you, please connect with a therapist to work through that healing process.

FAILURE/SUCCESS ANALYSIS

In this section of your work, you are going to utilize the **Failure/Success Analysis Tool** to approach past failures through reflection. This will likely trigger some of the same feelings you have worked so hard to avoid, but now you understand those feelings have value and are here to deliver a message. Let's get that message, but stop being tripped up by past failures. You are turning past failure from a stumbling block into a stepping stone. I just want to make you aware of the emotions that may come up. If you've done the work in Part I, you've developed the skills you'll need to process uncomfortable feelings. When used this way, this exercise will help your brain reflect on failure in order to notice important patterns, beliefs, and actions that make a difference in the results you create. This is a type of mental contrasting through which you create awareness of two different outcomes to capture valuable learning and understand how you can stand on the shoulders of your past self.

In this model, first, let's get clear on the example of failure you are using to explore. You have already made a list of past failures, and you can absolutely choose something from it to explore more deeply. However, in this process of approaching failure, other instances of failure may have come to mind, or you may be resisting this work altogether. Remember: Humans are masters at avoiding uncomfortable feelings, so you may have to take some time to connect with an example of failure in your past. When have you applied for something you didn't get? What promising relationships didn't work out the way you'd hoped? What goals have you failed to achieve? I know this may feel like a downer exercise, but while you should expect to feel resistance from your brain, frame this activity instead like a treasure hunt. You are searching for value.

Your brain may take a couple of paths here. It can resist looking at this failure because the emotions tied to it make you uncomfortable and are therefore a threat. It cannot accurately discern this memory from a new experience of failure, and according to your brain, failure could be fatal and should be avoided. Alternatively, your brain may take the path of ruminating on this failure (playing it on a loop in your memory) to make sure you recognize future threats. Because it has labeled that experience as a threat, it may feel the best way to protect you is to support the idea that the risk of repeating the circumstance of failure is death. Either way, your brain is working to protect you with the tools it has. However, you know how to boss your brain, and you have different tools to keep moving toward how you want to show up in the world. Use the skills we talked about in our first permission. With kind, compassionate self-talk, tell yourself that this is an empowering observation.

One thing some of my clients have found helpful when working through this model is to picture themselves as diamond miners. You've got the tools you need, and you're all geared up to go looking in a dark, cold, uncomfortable mine for diamonds. In much the same way, you are unearthing diamonds from your past experiences to help you see the value in those experiences and carry that value forward to enrich your present and future life.

Or you can picture yourself as Indiana Jones, looking to uncover valuable antiquities that can teach you about past lives. This is a treasure hunt, my friend. Sometimes, my clients make this mindset more concrete with the help of a structure or an artifact. This just means leveraging a physical object to connect you with a desired mindset. This could be something you treasure, like a loved one's watch that has been passed down to you or a vintage book you tracked down to complete your collection. Set the object on a desk or table where you are working. Or you could choose an item you actually put on that helps you feel like Indiana Jones—a great hat or some perfectly broken-in hiking boots. You don't need to go and buy something for this. It is, in fact, more effective to choose something that you have a strong emotional attachment to already. This technique is often used by athletes to get themselves into flow. Like you, they are not trying, they are training. Using a structure helps you reconnect with emotions that support your chosen mindset.

Now it's time to choose a past failure to explore. This brave exploration is part of approaching failure. It not only builds your tolerance muscle but also shows you another tool to get the best learning from failure, as well as rewiring your thinking habits about failure. Because you can do this as much as you want, you might want to focus first on a failure that doesn't incite a strong emotional response and, over time, work up to a more intense example. With your chosen example, clarify what your original intention was in this situation.

Let's say you applied for a job and didn't get it. Your original intention was to get the job. Be aware that there are some situations when the failure does not rest on you, but you will closely examine the circumstance in the context of the actions you can control or influence.

INTENTION: GET A NEW JOB

What does success look like?

- Submitting applications to jobs that align with my values
- Showing up well in interviews
- Getting a job that supports my goals and values and pays my bills

What choices/actions would make success possible?

- Update resume
- Build connections
- Research target
- Submit and follow up on applications
- Prep for interview
- Get the job and create value

What does failure look like?

- Not applying for anything
- Staying ignorant of valuable connections
- Not getting an interview
- Not paying my bills
- Staying where I am

What choices/actions would make failure probably?

- Use a non-targeted or outdated resume
- No research on potential organizations
- Only applying for one job
- Never following up on applications
- Not prepping for interviews
- Not seeking development that makes me valuable for desired position/field

First, write your original intention at the top. Since you are already looking at this past experience as a failure, the most easily accessed portion of the model is the lower left quadrant: What did failure look like? You probably visited this vision multiple times when you initially processed this experience. What about this experience told you it was a failure? Hint: It should include the opposite of your original intention.

Next, look at what success in the context of this experience would have looked like at that time. Here is the thing about doing this sort of mental contrast on something from the past: You may already be able to see how this failure has served your present self well. For instance, think about someone you might have married but the relationship didn't work out in the end—you may now have lived enough that you understand that person would have been a partner with very different goals and values from yours. However, for the sake of this exercise, stand in your original intention to get your past self's perspective on success. At that time, what would you have said success looked like? Hint: It should include your original intention.

I have heard some coaches who do similar work claim that by doing this type of exercise, you are actually changing your past failures. You are not changing the facts; rather, you are changing your *perspective* on them in order to notice valuable lessons that might have previously been hidden underneath uncomfortable emotions and therefore avoided. Remember that you have permission to approach.

Now that you have a clear picture of what both success and failure look like in the context of your original intention, write down what behaviors you exhibited in that circumstance that made the failure probable. If you are struggling to be objective, I've found that one thing that helps is to act as if this were an analysis of another person's failure. Be sure that the person who failed is someone you love. Let's say a young person you love, like a niece, nephew, daughter, or goddaughter, comes to you to process this failure. What would you lovingly help them notice about the choices they made that led to failure? This is what you want to be able to do for yourself.

For the last quadrant in the tool, look at what actions would have made success possible. You may already have processed these thoughts in the form of self-flagellation. Think about the "if only I had . . ." moments in your internal conversation. Be careful not to step into self-judgment; we're exploring and learning here. Depending on the situation you are working with, you could also seek feedback from someone else who was involved. For example, when I have a client who applied for a job, didn't get the job, and can't figure out why, I have them reach out to the interviewer in a respectful way and ask for feedback: What could they have done better? What gaps showed up to them? What additional skills should they acquire? Also, notice that you may have done some of these things to try to better your chances of success. Just because you didn't succeed doesn't mean everything you did was wrong. We're looking to adjust, not necessarily to do a complete overhaul. What steps did you take, or could you have taken, to ensure you achieved the picture of success that you were aiming for?

Finally, looking at the chart you just created, answer a few questions:

- What surprised you in this exercise?

- If you were giving your future self advice, what lessons would you want to share from this exercise?

- Using the example of the aforementioned Failure/Success Analysis, what advice would you give the person (your past self or the close friend or family member you envisioned) who filled this out?

Be sure to capture your answers in your journal or your permissions notes on your phone. Writing it down helps cement your learning and gives you the ability to reflect and remember later. Don't waste the work. Learning without application just makes you a vault of knowledge instead of a vessel of impact. Now that you have worked to uncover the lessons and given advice to your future self, how can you apply those lessons in your current life? To get a better understanding of how to set your actions, take a look at the following example of how one of my clients applied this learning.

How to Learn from It Every Time

Becca wanted to be a professional soccer player. She had played all of her life and went to college on a soccer scholarship. Her undergrad degree was in engineering, but she really wanted to play at a professional level. It had been her goal from the first time she saw professional women's soccer on television. She trained hard, worked with her college coaches, and went to camps to get noticed by recruiters. The summer of her junior year of college, she tried out for a professional team and was not chosen. She was devastated.

This is about the time we started working together. It felt like she had paid her dues, worked hard, and come up against a roadblock that marked the end of her dreams. We explored to uncover how she wanted to move forward. We looked at her values, passions, strengths, and weaknesses. She didn't want to give up her dream of professional soccer, but she also recognized, based on the feedback from her last tryout, that her physical size was an obstacle. In our work on her passions, I asked her what she loved most about soccer. At first, Becca said that she loved the team aspect; the excitement of pushing yourself to your physical, mental, and emotional limits; and the mentoring she had received and given to other players and coaches.

Then as we looked more closely at these elements, she said, "I like being an example of a strong, smart, and skilled woman." I asked her to think about other areas where she shows up as an example of a strong, smart, and skilled woman. She smiled and said, "Well, at school, I'm at the top of my program and have had some offers for internships next year."

"Where else?" I asked.

"I coach my niece's soccer team. I guess I'm an example for them." I asked if she would like to unpack this a little more. When she said yes, we worked through this Failure/Success Analysis Tool. After completing the analysis, her learnings were that working hard and pursuing a dream builds mental and emotional muscle. She learned that the uncomfortable emotions she was experiencing from her recent failure were delivering the message that she cared about her dreams. She also uncovered her belief that she could do anything if she worked hard enough. When we explored further, she saw that this belief both supported her goals and contributed to her feeling of disappointment. We worked on replacing it with a stronger and more accurate belief: "You can try anything if you work hard enough." We combined that with: "Every intentional attempt yields value." From this, the advice she gave to her future self was: "You know how to work hard at something. Make sure you are focused on all the ways you can lean into your values, strengths, and passion. Uncomfortable feelings are okay and bring you important information. Don't waste that information—learn from it every time."

The actions Becca set to make sure she was learning from these circumstances were to keep up with her soccer, still work with coaches to improve her game, and try out again after her senior year of college. She also committed to scaling back some of her additional soccer work to accept a lucrative internship, applying to grad school, and noticing every day that she is intentional about continuing to become a strong, smart, and skilled woman. Notice how working through the Failure/Success Analysis Tool can support learning and applying the lessons of failure.

At this point, you've done a lot of work in approaching, adjusting, and acting on your permission to fail. Let's do a self-compassion check. How are you? Building momentum? Feeling overwhelmed? Losing interest? Maintaining the status quo? Remember to notice those feelings. You may have to spend a lot of time and energy approaching this work but remember also that part of your permission is to adjust your pace, your practice, your support, and your goals. From this place of self-compassion, what do you need?

Just check in with yourself before you continue. Was part of the journey really challenging? Do you need to spend more time on some of these tools to aid you with a certain skill or struggle? Do you need to get a coach to support you in that work? Was a wound revealed and working with a therapist feels like a supportive next step? Make sure that as you perform this self-check, you set *actions* for yourself. It's the third principle that keeps you moving forward. Even if the action is to take a break and just practice one particular tool, set an additional action of putting a date on your calendar as a reminder to restart your work on these permissions.

My friends, I hope you will play with the Failure/Success Analysis Tool. While this is not a tool you will necessarily use the moment you encounter failure, the intentional learning this process yields will inform your actions as you pursue your goals. If you are waning in motivation, reflect on the science of failure. Those who are the best learners from failure increase their success potential.

TAKEAWAYS

- **Analyzing past failures provides essential information** on the journey of giving yourself permission to fail. But looking back on past failures can be emotionally taxing, and most avoid doing so. As a result, **before you can learn from past failures, you must first give yourself permission to approach**—not avoid—their memories.

- Use the **Failure/Success Analysis Tool** to approach past failures through reflection. Choose a past failure and work through the questions in each quadrant to uncover valuable takeaways from that experience of failure.

- It's important to **use the lessons of failure to spur concrete action in your life**, otherwise you will become a vault of knowledge instead of a vessel of impact. Those who are the best learners from failure increase their success potential.

10

Practicing the Permission to Fail

When you look up the word "practice" in the dictionary, you will notice that it is both a noun and a verb. Even more interesting, all forms of the definition contain an element of regular, systematic, or continual application. To be proficient, make continual impact, and grow in your permissions, you must both practice consistently and cultivate a practice that skillfully leverages tools to achieve your goals while aligning with your values.

Reflect on the general principles of permission—approach, adjust, and act. I want to make sure you leave Part II with everything you need to act. As you conclude this portion of our permissions journey, make sure you are noticing how you can practice your new skills. I want to bring back an old friend from our first permission to help you practice failure.

Remember the FETBO Template? I think the best tools are the ones that perform multiple tasks. When my friend undertook her journey to traverse the Grand Canyon, she had to think carefully about everything she carried with her, knowing that these items would weigh her down. What could she carry that could multitask, eliminating the need to carry multiple single-use items? One item could have been her trail map. Because it was laminated, it could hold up to being used as a fan, a small temporary shade, a vessel to catch or scoop water in a pinch, and probably serve a few other functions too. It was a multipurpose item and so is the FETBO Template. Remember that you used this tool after you allowed and discerned the message of an uncomfortable emotion to help you adjust your focus to different emotions that could serve you better. The FETBO Template can be just as useful as you practice permission to fail.

APPLYING THE FETBO TEMPLATE

To use the FETBO Template in practicing the permission to fail, instead of starting with the emotion line, start with the outcome line. The goal here is to uncover and adjust the thoughts and emotions that supported the failing outcome. How is this different from the Failure/Success Analysis Tool? Using the analysis tool, you were looking to uncover what elements worked and didn't work in your attempt to create results—that means actions, support, preparation, and information. With the FETBO Template, you are looking to understand what thoughts and emotions supported the actions you took. Remember: You are learning from failure and recognizing the value of those experiences. Keep in mind that not all aspects of failure are in your control. While you don't want to shift into blame, you also don't want to carry the load of other people's processes or external circumstances. You just want to notice what you can shift in your own thoughts and emotions to support a more successful outcome. This requires data that you can get from this exploration.

Use the same failure outcome you noticed in your work with the Failure/Success Analysis. Do this the first time using your FETBO Template regarding failure because the two models should prove each other in our work here. You don't have to do this every time you use the FETBO Template, but it's a great way to build proficiency. So for now, let's use the same example from the previous chapter of applying for a job and not getting it.

On the outcome line, put a sentence that captures what the failure looked like. Just a reminder, when using the FETBO Template, first address the lines that are the low-hanging fruit, meaning the easiest to fill in. The order is not set in stone—what is easy for one person is not so easy for another.

The next easiest items may be the facts line. For our example, let's fill in the facts that match that outcome. In this case, "I have a job. I pay my bills." These are the provable circumstances. You might be tempted to say things like, "I'm unhappy all the time," "I don't want to get out of bed," or "I never get to travel because I don't have the money." While you might be able to argue that these are circumstances, this line needs to be populated by provable facts—able to be observed by someone outside of the situation.

Now let's go for the behaviors line. This time through, you can again look at your Failure/Success Analysis. What actions did you describe that made failure probable? On the behaviors line, record an action that you feel was the biggest contributor or that you notice brings up emotions when you reflect on the situation.

Next, fill in the E line with the emotions you felt at the time or that come up for you when you recall the actions that created this outcome of failure.

Finally, fill in the thoughts. Remember that you can do these before tackling the emotions if you like. Some people access their thoughts more easily than feelings. Ask yourself, what thoughts were on replay during this time? If you can't remember, step more deeply into your observer role by looking at all the other lines you have filled in. What do you think a person with this outcome, in these facts, choosing these behaviors, and experiencing these feelings would be thinking? Your imagination will get you close if not spot-on with the thoughts you were carrying at that time.

F	Facts—Provable circumstances
E	Emotion—Feelings about the circumstances
T	Thoughts—Thinking about the circumstances
B	Behaviors—Actions in the circumstances
O	Outcome—The results you created by your actions

Let's work through the FETBO Template based on the Failure/Success Analysis you did in the last section. Notice how you can use this tool to adjust based on the outcome of the failure. In this context you already know the failure, so start with the Outcome line on the template.

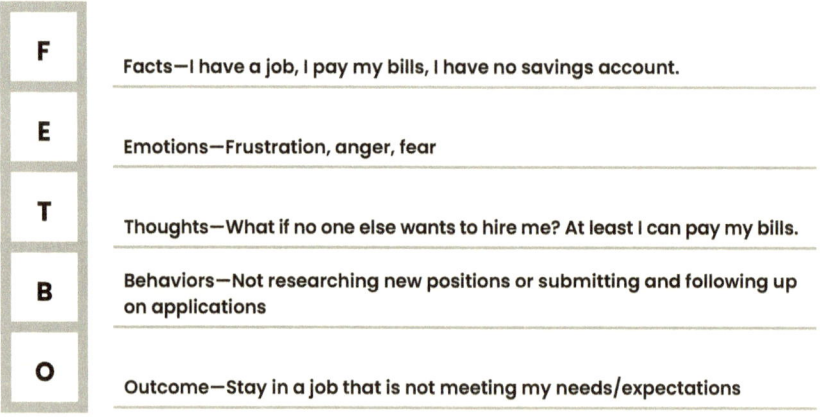

F	Facts—I have a job, I pay my bills, I have no savings account.
E	Emotions—Frustration, anger, fear
T	Thoughts—What if no one else wants to hire me? At least I can pay my bills.
B	Behaviors—Not researching new positions or submitting and following up on applications
O	Outcome—Stay in a job that is not meeting my needs/expectations

In this example, what do you think would be the lessons learned? Actually, generate a few lessons on your own before you keep reading. You are using every opportunity to learn from failure. Here are a few that I generated from this model:

- Focusing on my fear does not motivate me to act in a way that supports my goals.
- Sometimes I mistake gratitude for contentment, which inspires me to stay safe.
- When I am frustrated, angry, and fearful, I avoid proactive responses.
- Inaction creates a static impact. If I do nothing, nothing changes.

I want you to notice that these examples of lessons learned are all in the present tense. Even though you are looking at a past outcome, you want to apply the lessons to your current circumstance, so frame them that way.

Past: Focusing on my fear did not motivate me to act in a way that supported my goals.

Present: Focusing on my fear does not motivate me to act in a way that supports my goals.

Now let's flip the script on the lessons learned. Play with changes that are not only present tense but focus on what to do versus what not to do. Explore inserting opposites to see if they help you craft a more proactive lesson statement. For example:

Original lesson: Focusing on my fear does not motivate me to act in a way that supports my goals.

Proactive version: Focusing on energizing emotions helps me act in a way that supports my goals.

How can the FETBO Template help you apply permission to fail in your present? At the beginning of this permission, I told you a story about my daughter's tennis coach—how he gave them permission to lose the match but not to quit playing their game. Following is an example of what it would look like to work through the FETBO Template before and after he gave them that permission.

BEFORE PERMISSION TO FAIL

F	Facts—I am losing to a skilled opponent.
E	Emotions—Embarrassed with my performance; shame about letting my partner and team down.
T	Thoughts—I cannot lose this match.
B	Behaviors—I will play cautiously and try not to make mistakes.
O	Outcome—I lose points and focus on not losing more.

AFTER PERMISSION TO FAIL

F	Facts—I am losing to a skilled opponent.
E	Emotion—Hopeful about playing better; confident because I'm learning.
T	Thoughts—I'm an experienced tennis player and continue to improve.
B	Behaviors—Focus on tennis foundations and my strengths; make mental notes about what to work on.
O	Outcome—I am showing up, playing to my strengths, and giving my best effort.

Notice that the facts did not change, but everything else did. To fill out and compare similar templates for your own situation, one for which you have not performed a Failure/Success Analysis because it is "real time," it is often easiest to first fill in the facts line. What are the facts of this present situation where you are not exercising permission to fail? Remember that you are not changing anything yet, just exploring a current situation.

Then, the next most accessible line to complete is likely the emotions line. This is especially true if you have been working on your feelings fitness and are now skilled at noticing and labeling your emotions.

Work through each line for your current situation. Next, work through it again, but be mindful—you can approach, adjust, and act with permission here. Ask yourself, "If I had permission to fail, what would look different on this model?" Start with the easy one—the facts of the circumstance should be the same as you listed the first time. Next, fill in your desired outcome. What outcome do you want to create? Then look at the emotions line—if you had permission to fail in this outcome, what emotions would you experience? What thoughts would you hold? What behaviors would you choose? What could the outcome look like based on those actions?

Circle back with me to see how the template changes with permission to fail at finding a job:

F	Facts—I have a job, I pay my bills, I have no savings account.
E	Emotions—Freedom, hope, curiosity
T	Thoughts—What jobs are out there that excite me, where can I add value, and that exceed my needs?
B	Behaviors—Build my contacts with people who do exciting work; do my research on how to do what they do; consistently send in applications to multiple exciting organizations
O	Outcome—Enjoy the process and find a new job that will help me grow personally and professionally

Again, notice what did and didn't change from the first run-through. What would be your lessons learned here? How about, "When I feel free, hopeful, and curious, I take actions that are exciting and create desirable impact?" This feels easy when I present a completed template, but now it is time for you to get working on completing your own template. It will be challenging, and it will get easier the more you do it.

This practice will help you continue to learn lessons from failure, adjust your mindset to see the value in the experiences, and make adjustments in current circumstances with the lens of permission to fail. Have a look at another example.

BEFORE PERMISSION TO FAIL

F	Facts—At a party with a lot of people
E	Emotions—Frustrated; embarrassed; awkward
T	Thoughts—I'm not interesting enough; I can't think of anything to say.
B	Behaviors—Stay quiet; move to the outer edge of the room; play with my phone
O	Outcome—I spend the evening doing what I could have done at home.

This template is based on the experiences of several of my clients who were frustrated in their efforts to be more social and expand relationships. The frustration of making the effort of attending a large function with social goals, only to end up spending that time by themselves instead, is real. With one client, once we worked through the template the first time, I asked them, when they thought those thoughts and felt those emotions, were they surprised by the behaviors they chose or the outcomes those behaviors created? They were not surprised by the outcome but were surprised by the ways the template showed the connections.

We already knew the outcome they wanted to create—more social interaction and relationships—so the next time we filled in the template, we put that outcome in the O line. Then I asked my clients how they would feel about this outcome. Sometimes, it helps to step back into observer mode and ask: What would someone who creates that outcome be feeling? This helps to uncover desirable emotions that support the wanted outcome. Then, because my clients and I build emotional literacy and a Library of Emotions before we practice the FETBO Template, in this context, we can put on those emotions and ask what thoughts someone with those emotions might be thinking with those facts. And finally, what would someone thinking these thoughts and feeling these emotions choose to do to create their desired outcome? Here is what their second time through the FETBO Template might look like.

AFTER PERMISSION TO FAIL

F	Facts—At a party with a lot of people
E	Emotions—Helpful, engaged, confident
T	Thoughts—I can help others feel interesting.
B	Behaviors—Plan a few questions ahead of time and watch for opportunities to help others shine
O	Outcome—I interact and build connections by learning a lot about the people at the party.

Great work! Hopefully, our efforts with the FETBO Template feel more familiar this second time around. You already practiced this tool in Part I of the book, and now you can see how it can be helpful as you take action based on your learnings from experiences of failure. Consistent practice will increase your skill and effectiveness with this tool.

CHECKING IN

Within the practice section of each permission, I incorporate ways to measure your progress on this journey. Check in on where you are on the following Permission to Fail Map.

Image 6.1: Permission to Fail Map

Assess yourself. Rate how strongly you agree with each statement on a scale of 1–10, with 1 being "I strongly disagree" and 10 being "I strongly agree."

- I can approach situations of failure without incapacitating anxiety.

- I no longer avoid situations where failure is a possibility.

- I can process the emotions that go with failure.
- I can analyze situations where I have failed and glean valuable lessons from the uncomfortable situation.
- I agree that experiencing failure is valuable.
- I can make adjustments to situations where I feel like I'm failing by giving myself permission to fail, which changes my thoughts, feelings, actions, and outcomes without a change in circumstances.
- I have a growth mindset of humility, which helps me continue to learn and grow personally and professionally.

Pay attention to the areas where you rated yourself with low numbers. What could you do to bump that number up by one? Possibly take a break from the work or revisit the sections of this permission that need a boost according to your measure.

As a tip, do not overlook the power of reflection. It is the most important tool that allows us to learn from both success and failure. You can use these tools as part of your reflection time or you can simply conduct a brief "after-action review," a term borrowed from the military. After each strategic move, take time to ask yourself:

- What worked?
- What didn't work?
- What advice would I give my past self, based on my results?

Be sure to record your reflections so you can stand on the shoulders of your past self.

Congratulations! You are about to embark on the third leg of this journey. I know you took measure of how you feel you have done in giving yourself permission to fail, but I want you to take a moment and celebrate your effort. Even if you are just reading the book without stopping to do work with the tools, you are expanding awareness and investing in becoming a person who is in partnership with their feelings and can leverage failure with the humility and resilience to keep working toward creating the positive impact this world needs. Well done!

One more thing I want to check in on: Are you taking this journey solo? Back to my hiking friend—while she did her trek alone, she also had a lot of support from her partner who encouraged her, drove her to one rim, manned the phone for signals in case she needed to check in, and picked her up at the other rim of the Grand Canyon. I'm cheering you on as you go, but I also hope you have invited someone in your life to encourage you on this journey. If not, with whom could you share your time in these pages? Just a conversation about what you've learned and how you are planning to apply it can be all it takes for someone to encourage you.

All right, fellow travelers, it's time to fly!

TAKEAWAYS

- The best tools are the ones that perform multiple tasks. The **FETBO Template** is such a tool and **can also be used in practicing the permission to fail.**
- **Working through the FETBO Template** from the perspective of a past failure will help you continue to **learn lessons from failure, adjust your mindset to see the value in the experiences, and make adjustments in current circumstances** with the lens of permission to fail.
- **Take a moment and celebrate your effort.** You are expanding awareness and investing in becoming a person in partnership with their feelings, who can leverage failure with humility and resilience to keep working toward creating the positive impact this world needs. Well done!

PART III

Permission to Fly

Mission Mindset: Flying is a **process** that takes belief, action, learning, strategy, and time.

> *The moment you doubt whether you can fly, you cease forever to be able to do it. So come with me, where dreams are born, and time is never planned. Just think of happy things, and your heart will fly on wings, forever, in Never Never Land!*
>
> —J.M. BARRIE,
> THE COMPLETE ADVENTURES OF PETER PAN

Flying for Peter Pan meant freedom, escape, and joy. And J.M. Barrie was onto something: Flying is about belief. However, I think Barrie also nailed a false belief that can get in the way of our flying. Humans often associate dreams with serendipity versus strategy or with lots of hard work and little joy. And there is that either-or thinking. Not achieving your dream success? You're just unlucky or you're not working hard enough. And trusting only happy thoughts might get you to the imaginary Neverland, but they can cause blind spots that actually prevent you from creating the impact and results you envision. Barrie spoke of these blind spots and labeled them lack of belief when he wrote, "In time they could not even fly after their hats. Want of practice, they called it; but what it really meant was that they no longer believed." I actually believe lack of flight is down to a combination of lacking belief *and* "want of practice." More specifically, those who struggle to fly no longer hold beliefs that support flight and they do not even try to practice flying. I know I am talking about a work of fiction, but so often, fiction illustrates powerful aspects of the human condition. As you work on applying the permission principles to flying, you will put strategy to dreaming, continue to build skills that help to adopt supportive beliefs, and practice, practice, practice the application of these skills.

Remember: The truth is actually in the tension of approaching thoughts and feelings that you instinctively want to avoid. Notice the tension between dreaming—which people often forget how to do—and working with supportive beliefs to make our dreams reality. See the tension between positive, happy thoughts and looking for data and blind spots that could prevent success. You have spent many pages learning how to approach, adjust, and act. I invite you to apply that learning and those principles to flight.

11

Planning to Fly: Flying Map

Before you take off, do a quick check-in on your journey, determine your bearings, and get ready to put the permission principles to work.

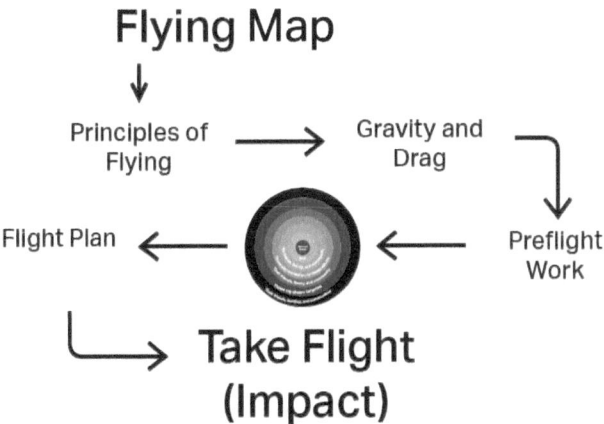

Image 11.1: Permission to Fly Map

When it comes to permission, "flying" means pursuing dreams, creating impact, and achieving success in your endeavors. Though success is subjective, it looks like having a lot of money for some, helping people live their dreams for others, living without the constraint of physical trappings for still others. Depending on your values, it could be a combination of these things or anything else. However you define success, you experience feelings of success when you are aligned with your values and moving toward your vision.

Why do you long for flight? Based on the aforementioned definition, flying means pursuing dreams, creating impact, and achieving success. Let me ask you: If you felt that definition reflected your life right now, would you feel happy? I want to bring this into our conversation because I do not want you to buy into the "grass is greener" syndrome. This ailment happens when you believe that if you just do, accomplish, or attain a certain goal, you'll be happy.

When you suffer from this, your happiness is a moving target—something you work for, not something you are. To be clear, I don't want you to long for flight because then you'll be happy. While this pursuit of happiness is a motivator for some, it can make happiness feel transactional: "I do this, so I have earned a certain amount of happiness. I achieve this and get happiness in return." This transactional mindset means that sometimes, people don't allow themselves happiness because they don't feel that they've earned it. However, you already have permission to be happy. In case you didn't notice, that is a being identifier. So if happiness is not why you long for flight, why even do this work? Let's circle back to our definition of flight.

- You long for flight because you enjoy dreaming and pursuing those dreams. It gives you purpose and motivation.
- You long for flight because you want to create an impact that prospers yourself, your community, and your planet.
- You long for flight because the fist-pump moment of achievement is thrilling.

Okay, hopefully, you now have more clarity on why flying is valuable to you. To benefit from that value, you will apply the principles of permission to flying. I want to remind and empower you to **approach**, **adjust**, and **act** to pursue dreams, create impact, and achieve success. What does this really look like? In this permission, we'll examine how to use the tools to reconnect with your dreams and notice how to approach those dreams in small choices that shift your trajectory in the desired direction. Bravely look at the tension between what you envision your actions will accomplish and what your current actions are actually creating. Then you can make adjustments as needed. Additionally, you will learn from your own failures and those of others to formulate and take strategic, consistent actions.

My hiking friend had a vision to stay active, challenge herself, and spend quality time with her family. Here is something I have not shared about her Grand Canyon hike: One of her family members was supposed to go with her but had to back out a couple of weeks before the big journey. This caused her to reevaluate the true meaning of the trip for her. This was supposed to be a time to push herself while supporting and being supported by a dear loved one. She still had the tools and strategy, the knowledge of the trail, the lessons learned from the journeys of others, as well as her own physical training. She chose to continue with her trek alone not because of "sunk cost"—what she had already invested in the hike—but because it still aligned with her values. She would be challenging herself even more without the safety net of a younger, stronger companion. To accommodate the new challenge, she added some check-in points with a family member who would drop her off at the start and wait for her to ascend at the end. She kept **approaching** her vision, but she took a hard look at her beliefs about herself and **adjusted** her strategies. Then she took bold **action.**

For our work, before you jump into adjustment and action, let's approach a little deeper by looking at the challenges of flying, otherwise known as gravity and drag.

TAKEAWAYS

- When it comes to permission, **flying means pursuing dreams, creating impact, and achieving success** in your endeavors.

- There are **three reasons you long to fly:**
  1. Because you enjoy dreaming and pursuing those dreams. It gives you purpose and motivation.
  2. Because you want to create an impact that prospers yourself, your community, and your planet.
  3. Because the fist-pump moment of achievement is thrilling.

- Examine the **tension between your current actions and the actions that would actually bring you closer to achieving your dreams.** What adjustments can you make to get yourself back on track?

12

Gravity and Drag of Flight

With the first two permissions, you explored the value of knowing the challenges of that specific permission. This practice is even more important in the permission to fly. In the flight plan for an airplane, the pilot must account for things that challenge flight—like gravity and drag. It's no different in preparing for permission to fly in your life. In this chapter, you will continue looking at different aspects of the same challenges we looked at previously—blame, self-trust, passivity, and identity—with the lens of how they apply to our flight.

BLAME

As you turn your attention to success, consider the role of a particular cognitive bias, which is basically the blame habit with a little finesse. This is called the self-serving bias. Psychologists define it as "the tendency to interpret events in a way that assigns credit for success to oneself but denies one's responsibility for failure, which is blamed on external factors. The self-serving bias is regarded as a form of self-deception designed to maintain high self-esteem."[1] Or as Steven Covey interpreted this concept, "We judge ourselves by our intentions and others by their behavior."[2] Pretty much what we've already covered, but let's dig a little deeper and notice how having a self-serving bias affects our flight by informing both judgmentalism and judgment.

First, let's look at being judgmental to make sure we're clear on what that means in these pages. Here, being judgmental means forming mostly disparaging or disapproving opinions with limited time, perspective, and energy. You've already done the work to notice how often you slip into blaming. Now I'd like you to notice how often you find yourself judging others. Why and how is this part of self-serving bias? When you judge others, you notice things from the perspective that your opinion or way of doing things is superior, and self-serving bias gives evidence that you are indeed superior. After all, if all our success happens because you are smarter, faster, bolder, or brighter than others and all our failures are because of unfortunate circumstances, mechanical failure, or the stupidity of others, then aren't you superior? (If, at this point, I need to tell you this is my form of sarcasm, you might need to pause here and start the book over.) But I hope that you see how self-serving bias undergirds judgmentalism.

So, is judgmentalism bad? Some would claim that it is a moral downfall. I am not here to debate the moral side of judgmentalism, but I am here to help you see that it is detrimental to your success. Consider the following:

- Being judgmental will close your mind to the contributions of others. You will miss valuable insights because you have judged the messenger and their message.
- Being judgmental will expose areas where you feel insecure, undermining your self-confidence and self-trust.
- Being judgmental can empower blind spots about your strengths and weaknesses.
- Being judgmental will hamper your ability to connect with others and subvert relationships that create meaning.

- Because being judgmental draws on your past experiences through a self-serving lens, it curtails future vision and innovation.
- Being judgmental is basically rewarding our brains for seeking negative attributes of ourselves, others, and circumstances.

Sounds like being judgmental creates pretty big challenges, right? In her work on question thinking, Marilee Adams, author and founder of the Inquiry Institute, says, "With a Judger mindset, the costs can be tremendous. The future can be only a recycled version of the past."[3] The past is not where we're aiming as you work to take flight. Okay, we've looked at these challenges, but how do you know if you are in a "judger mindset"?

You might be judgmental if you:

- Are repelled by those who aren't like you
- Believe everyone is an opponent or looking to take advantage of you
- Believe people and or their ideas are all good or all bad
- Start sentences with "I can't believe [object of judgmental] did/said/wore/thought/was with . . ."
- Find yourself frequently lamenting that someone is "always" a certain way, where the complaint is something derogatory and unlike you

So, how do you break free from this thinking habit that is judgmentalism? First, notice when your inner judge shows up. Second, similar to what you did with your feelings, get curious. Yes, it is activating a different part of the brain, but it also builds our empathy for others. What could that person's story be? What battle are they fighting that is causing them to show up as they are? What experiences could support their perspective? If your judgment is aimed toward yourself, exercise self-compassion—use your endearment and remind yourself that you are human and a work in progress. Then look for facts about this situation. This would be a great opportunity to dust off that FETBO Template and get to work. However your inner judge shows up, focus first on growth, not punishment; getting it right, not *being* right; and the problem, not the person.

Before you leave this vein of the blame challenge, let's also explore how the self-serving bias affects judgment—not with respect to being judgmental but when it comes to exercising judgment. If judgment is the ability to evaluate information and circumstances to make good decisions, then seeing that information and those circumstances through a self-serving bias will rob us of perspectives and information that are vital to good choices. For example, if you have surrounded yourself with only people who share your same goals, values, and experiences, no one will ever offer opinions or perspectives different from your own. If you only collect data from preferred sources, algorithms and influencers will determine your world views. Making decisions with an unrestrained self-serving bias is basically outsourcing good judgment.

Here are some measures you can take to overcome self-serving bias and exercise good judgment.

Prioritize Listening

Focus relentless attention on those who are speaking, ask questions, and reflect back conclusions that are being expressed. I once had a client who was high up in the healthcare industry. I asked him, as I often ask my clients, to periodically reflect and share what from our work had created the most impact. After giving it some thought, he said that the most profound impact was in the area of communication. "My team connection has soared," he told me. "When they come to my office, my new habit is to physically turn my phone facedown, close my computer, lean in, ask open-ended questions, and then listen. I don't think my solutions or advice have changed, but, by listening, I learn and build connection. What's crazy is how quickly the change happened—just because I made the person talking feel heard." He believes his team has grown to trust him more and that he is a more empathetic, effective leader because of his decision to listen.

Gather Broad Data

Make it a point to explore many relevant sources and perspectives. Because algorithms determine so much of what we see these days, you have to be intentional about shifting your sources of information. You can feel like you are doing a fair job of looking at different perspectives when in reality, you don't realize you're in an information bubble. Be extra intentional when you are relying on other people who are like you for information. They may not be breaking out of their information bubble themselves but are bringing their biases to you as facts. The tricky thing is that data may genuinely be factual but you're only able to hear half the facts. Pay attention to make sure you are critically considering the data and its sources.

Value Diversity over Validation

Be careful not to only look for confirmation of what you already believe. Not only should your data be diverse but your inner circle should be as well. One of my husband's favorite books is *Team of Rivals* by Doris Kearns Goodwin about one of his favorite leaders, Abraham Lincoln. Like my partner, I've always admired Lincoln for his understanding of paradoxical values, which I believe helped him overcome self-serving bias in his judgment. Lincoln was gentle yet bold, empathetic and direct, and wise but always learning. One of the greatest examples of Lincoln's paradoxes is who he turned to for counsel. In the book, Goodwin explores how Lincoln surrounded himself with those who had opposed him politically—people he believed were smart and whose experiences provided different views. Goodwin says, "Good leadership requires you to surround yourself with people of diverse perspectives who can disagree with you without fear of retaliation."[4] Good judgment calls for diverse perspectives as well.

Consider Your Close Counselors

The cost of cultivating good judgment is the comfort of surrounding yourself with those who will validate your perspective. It is a small price to pay. As you reflect on overcoming the flight challenge of self-serving bias, think about Lincoln's team of rivals. These were people he knew did not agree with him. Now I don't believe these were Lincoln's only close counselors, but in that same spirit, think about who you keep close.

As part of a leadership course I teach at the University of Denver, I take my students through an exercise to help them create awareness about the diversity of their inner circle (or lack thereof) and what steps can be taken to invite in diverse perspectives. While I don't ask my students to share specific results of the exercise, I do ask them what they learned from it. In a recent class, the first student who responded said, "My learning is not that my inner circle isn't diverse, but that I don't have one." They realized that not having an inner circle made their growth as a leader more challenging than it needed to be.

I use a similar exercise with my clients who are working to create impact, but we call it the golden circle. A golden circle is not just who you trust to ask advice from. A golden circle supports you as you move forward but in multifaceted ways; you also receive objective perspectives, advice for your journey, and the opportunity to give back.

Here's the thing: You also need diversity in this circle. There will be commonalities, but there must be differences as well if you really want to leverage the counsel of those in your golden circle to cultivate good judgment. Do not confuse this with your network. This is an intimate group who may be part of your network but who are allowed much closer than the rest of the group.

Who should be invited into the circle?

MENTOR

Someone who is ahead of you on this journey and can share their stories of moving toward success and help you navigate your own path. In the metaphor of my hiking friend, a mentor is someone who has already taken the trail you want to travel. Do not take the idea that they share a path for being identical to you. If you choose someone in your same line of work or passion, I invite you to seek someone who has marked differences from you as well. This will support your desire to avoid blind spots as you work to fly.

ENCOURAGER

Someone who knows you and can remind you of your success. Your encourager should have some history with you. They are the person who can testify that you have faced other challenges, survived, and thrived.

MENTEE

Someone who helps you recognize how far you've come and who you can pour into with lessons of your experience. In our hiking metaphor, this is someone who wants to take a trail you have already traveled. Once again, even though you are mentoring this person, make sure there is a mix of both similarities and differences. You will learn from them as well. In fact, you may learn more from this relationship than any other.

COACH

Because coaches are trained to objectively help you recognize your strengths, clarify your goals, and strategize ways to minimize weaknesses, they will challenge your thinking on a regular basis. In the hiking metaphor, a coach understands the process of hiking and helps you identify your gaps, guides you through how to address those gaps, works with you to set goals, and holds you accountable.

SPIRITUAL GUIDE

Someone who guides you to tap into a power outside of yourself. This can be someone you know who has a spiritual practice that you admire or a teacher you want to learn from, even if you don't personally interact but follow their teachings.

CHAMPION

Someone in your organization who will pound the table if necessary to help you get opportunities to develop. This is another powerful place to seek diversity. This person needs to believe in you, but they are also someone who will advise you and be invested in your success. Cultivating diversity in this seat of your circle will ensure that you don't sacrifice good judgment for self-serving bias.

I have presented each role in the golden circle as a different person fitting a single spot, but some of the roles may overlap into one person. Also, you can have more than one person in each role but beware of inviting too many voices into your golden circle. And, like my students in class, strive for diversity in that circle. This will prevent you from developing blind spots in your perspectives.

SELF-TRUST

Let's circle back to the challenge of self-trust. In each permission, you have looked at how self-trust supports or undermines your actions. One of the most common challenges to success when it comes to self-trust is imposter syndrome. This condition is actually a feeling supported by beliefs that you do not deserve or haven't actually earned your success. Instead of noticing the results you have created, you chalk success up to luck or serendipity—being in the right place at the right time. You can feel overwhelmed by the idea that soon it will be found out that you don't know what you're doing and are not experienced enough to steer your own or your team's vision of impact. You can be nagged by the energy drain of presenting a successful image, so people won't find out the ugly truth that you don't know what you're doing. Here is the good news: People who experience imposter syndrome are people who are looking to create impact and move forward in their success—high achievers. So understand that you are in good company.[5]

Imposter Syndrome

According to an article published by the American Psychological Association, imposter syndrome refers to the inability of high-achieving individuals to internalize success—with a persistent belief that they are frauds.[6] This is why imposter syndrome is a challenge to giving ourselves permission to fly. If you don't believe you've been successful in the past, you lack evidence to trust that you can be successful going forward. You may have flown before, and when you reached your goal or moved up the ladder, you became exhausted trying to keep up the "façade" that you deserved to be there.

So how do you confront this challenge? First, make sure you are strong in feelings fitness. Staying with the picture of flying, think of this as a pre-flight check. Feeling like a fraud brings up many uncomfortable emotions, but with the tools and consistent practices from permission to feel, you can welcome and process the messages of those uncomfortable feelings. Second, make sure your identity anchors are firmly rooted in clear values and are more about your *being* than your *doing*.

These uncomfortable feelings will often come up while "in flight." For example, you've been promoted to a manager level, and while it has been your goal for a while, you suddenly feel like every word you say or move you make exposes your inexperience and unworthiness to be there.

You know that awareness is the beginning of all work, and you are expanding your awareness just by reading these paragraphs. Regarding the feelings of imposter syndrome though, let's apply our principles of permission. Instead of avoiding those feelings, let's approach them by noticing when they rise up. What triggers your imposter syndrome? Who are you with? Where are you? What is happening at the time? Study these details. Now let's adjust with the FETBO Template. What could imposter syndrome look like in the FETBO Template? Follow the usual steps:

1. What are the conditions when your imposter feelings erupt? Look for the *facts* right now.
2. You've labeled the feelings. Drop those in the *emotions* line of the template.
3. What are the *thoughts* that go with those emotions?
4. What actions (*behaviors*) are you taking when this occurs?
5. What *outcomes* are you creating?

Let's put that all together in an example:

F	Facts—Newly accepted into a prestigious grad school program
E	Emotions—Dread, fear, sense of defeat
T	Thoughts—What happens when people find out I don't belong here?
B	Behaviors—Play small; keep quiet; try not to draw attention
O	Outcome—I make little to no impression, exemplify no learning, experience diminished value from the program, don't develop my network socially or professionally.

Now let's leverage an adjusted version of the template. The facts don't change, but the adjustment creates very different outcomes. Don't forget that you can start the FETBO Template with whichever line feels most accessible, but once the facts are stated, sometimes it's easiest to just write down the outcome you desire and then fill in the next easiest line. For some items, you may have to ask yourself questions in the theoretical: What behaviors would create that outcome? What would one have to think to choose those behaviors? If one believed that thought, behaved that way, and created those outcomes, what would one feel? Play with the order to find the sequence that feels the most empowering. Here is what the adjusted template could look like:

F	Facts—Newly accepted into a prestigious grad school program
E	Emotions—Excitement, enthusiasm, sense of hope
T	Thoughts—I'm here to learn, not to know everything already; this is a great place to learn and meet others with similar interests.
B	Behaviors—Ask questions; seek discussion; try new things
O	Outcome—I acquire new knowledge, learn new applications, and exponentially increase my social and professional network.

It is important with imposter syndrome to notice the power of adjusting your thoughts. This is not a fake-it-till-you-make-it approach, but shifting to a believable, supportive thought can ramp up your power to fly when you're feeling like an imposter. I have found that sometimes my clients struggle to figure out the thought line of the FETBO Template, so I want to spend a little more time looking at the role our thoughts play in imposter syndrome.

Let's notice something that happens when our imposter syndrome feelings are triggered. Often your mind is invaded with **automatic negative thoughts (ANTs)**, a term and idea that originated with Dr. Daniel Amen.[7] It may take some work for you to notice ANTs because they are indeed automatic—our brain presents them, especially when our imposter syndrome feelings are triggered. It is at this point you will really begin to appreciate the adjustment chops you have built during our work together. ANTs happen quickly and are an indicator that you are not bossing your brain or practicing emotional fitness.

Since you identified your triggers for imposter syndrome earlier, take time to reflect on the last time you were triggered and examine that episode for these sneaky negative thoughts. Write a list of those thoughts that looped in your brain during that episode, on the left side of a piece of paper. Now it's time to kill some ANTs and replace them with **more accurate thoughts (MATs)**. For each negative thought you have written, check the facts. Are they true? Is there a more accurate thought that would support your identity anchors? Also notice our MATs are believable because they are based on facts. We're not going to settle for allowing ANTs to write stories that do not serve us.

Let's go back to our example of the newly promoted manager. Let's say the ANTs for this manager are:

- I have no idea how to do this job.

- When Sherry offered to answer any questions, it's because she knows I don't know what I'm doing.

- My team is not engaging with me because people think I'm incompetent.

- My boss will be coming to my office today to tell me they made a mistake and ask me to leave.

- I will never be comfortable in this position.

- They actually should fire me.

It's not enough to just notice the ANTs or even to simply say they aren't true. Picture this: Every spring at my home, I have a colony of ants, the actual little crawly kind, that decide to work their way under my front door and reside in the entryway of my home. I do not wish to share my home with ants, so tell me . . . how effective would it be to just notice that ants had invaded? No, you spray those ants, but you must also block their entry point until they learn they cannot come in. Yes, I duct tape my front door shut for a few days every spring.

Imposter syndrome ANTs must be tackled with just as much intention, effort, and creativity. With all the ANTs—automatic negative thoughts—recorded on the left side of your page, take each ANT and write a MAT—a more accurate thought—next to it based on what you know to be true. You're not just identifying and denying the verity of the ANTs, you are replacing them so they don't have space to reenter. Here's an example:

- I have no idea how to do this job. ➡ Actually, I know many aspects of the work my team does; I need to learn more about managing people.

- When Sherry offered to answer any questions, it's because she knows I don't know what I'm doing. ➡ Actually, Sherry is willing to be a resource for me.

- My team is not engaging with me because people think I'm incompetent. ➡ Actually, my team will engage more when people know me better and recognize that they can trust me.

- My boss will be coming to my office today to tell me they made a mistake and ask me to leave. ➡ Actually, my boss was new once too, and I could ask for their feedback and advice.

- I will never be comfortable in this position. ➡ Actually, being new is uncomfortable, but there will be a time when I am no longer new.

- They actually should fire me. ➡ Actually, my boss and coworkers know I'm new and will help me become what they need in a manager.

Practice! ANTs are part of life and will constantly provide you with the opportunity to practice more accurate thinking. Keep your list so that you can replace ANTs with MATs in your current situation. You can also use this list to help you populate your FETBO Template because your MATs can be powerful in your thought line. When needed, make a new list. Imposter syndrome may rise up with each new venture, but you don't have to dread it. You know how to manage this challenge and take flight.

Success Tip: Perform a Success Audit

Create an ongoing list of your successes. Take a few minutes and write down times when you felt really successful. Reflect on feedback you've received about what went well because of you and your intentional actions so that you can more easily internalize your success.

Think about a plane taking off. While there may be some lucky conditions that make it easier—i.e., clear skies and little wind—there is a lot of intention in the equipment design, fuel sources, instruments, skilled pilots, trained technicians, and engineers. A

> plane doesn't accidentally soar at 30,000 feet. Likewise, most of your success stands on the shoulders of intentional actions you have taken.

PASSIVITY

When you think about creating impact and succeeding in areas above or beyond your current results, does that mean constant striving? Constant action? Imagine the plate spinners in a Vaudeville act who run and dance while supporting spinning plates on poles to keep them from falling and breaking—entertaining but exhausting. These plate spinners are certainly active, but are they really getting anywhere? The issue of active versus passive behavior is more nuanced than simple good versus bad. Passivity has a place. Look through the lens of the entrepreneur and you might see an evergreen product that creates passive income—the holy grail of revenue without constant action. This kind of passivity is sought after, chosen. But passivity can be debilitating when it is an unconscious pattern of being—unhealthy when it's a default approach. Is there a healthy passivity? Remember: So often the truth is in the tension. The key here is intentionality, choosing when to be passive or active—or, in the well-known wisdom of Kenny Rogers' "The Gambler," knowing whether to hold or fold. There are circumstances and relationships that call for varying measures of passivity.

Popular podcast host, speaker, and author Mel Robbins went viral after proposing her "Let Them" theory, which she defines in the context of relationships as: "When you 'Let Them' do whatever it is that they want to do, it creates more control and emotional peace for you and a better relationship with the people in your life."[8] It is an interesting approach, and many have found benefits in its application. However (and I believe Robbins emphasizes this as well), while there is a time and a place when this approach is called for, it doesn't mean you are always passive. Personal boundaries still apply, and it is not a call for you to lay down as a doormat.

Thinking back to the analogy of the three buckets. The idea of letting others show up how they want to is a process of making sure you are not spending your energy stuffing people in your control bucket. With the exception of any very young children you may be guardian to, the only person in your control bucket is you. Through the seasons of parenting, you intentionally move your maturing children through a progression of each of your buckets. They are born in the control bucket, and, gradually, different areas of their lives move into the influence bucket, until they eventually move into your other bucket. All the while, you are teaching them how to handle their own three buckets.

Back to how passivity can show up in your control bucket. This idea is purposeful passivity. You choose where to apply a passive approach. There are times when you pause and just wait to see how something plays out. It is an intentional pause. There are times when you let people be who they are and let go of trying to force them into meeting your expectations. There are times when after communicating with each other about what you need, you may each rise to the occasion and meet the other's needs or you may let each other go. There are times when you have set the "plate" spinning and you experiment to see how long it can spin without giving it your constant energy. There are times when you choose not to take action because you don't have the resources of time, energy, and money to put toward it. There are times to be passive about something because putting your focus on it would pull focus away from something that is a higher value. There are times that call for purposeful passivity.

> **There are times that call for purposeful passivity.**

IDENTITY

Remember when you were young and someone asked you what you wanted to be when you grew up? Most likely, there were a lot of possibilities in your answer, all formed around some vision of what your six-year-old self wanted to do and be. Did you catch that? Starting from a young age, humans begin to merge doing and being identities. You might have said with full certainty that you wanted to be something like a firefighter–architect or a veterinarian–dentist. All of your limited years of experience kept you so open to answering with wild combinations of doing that grown-ups would smile and give you knowing nods.

When was the last time you asked a child, "What do you want to be when you grow up?" and they answered that they wanted to be kind, be a learner, be supportive? Now to be fair, when a child says they want to be a teacher, nurse, or doctor, they may be partially expressing the idea of being of service or caring for others. Still, the waters are murky between being and doing from an early age.

If you play out the metaphor of flying an airplane, dragging along an anchor sounds like a really bad idea. So pause the flight metaphor for a moment, please, and remember that an anchor is a tool that helps you stay in a chosen spot for as long as you desire, even when challenging circumstances buffet you. Anchoring only to doing identities can create a problem, as doing identities shift in different seasons and circumstances, while anchoring to being identities brings stability. So how is this a challenge to success?

Sometimes, what you anchor to creates drag that prevents you from envisioning how you want to impact the world. How can drag hamper vision? Drag keeps you tethered to or focused on one particular spot. Doing identities are important because they help you clarify what you put energy toward for yourself and others. That's why LinkedIn profiles are populated with doing identifiers: "Here is where I have worked to build expertise." Rarely do they contain words like "creative," "enthusiastic," or "generous." Instead, you use terms that express those forms of your identity, like "marketing manager," "human resources consultant," or "angel investor."

Doing anchors hamper your connection to vision and dreams outside of your roles, whereas being anchors can be pulled in and dropped down to support new, unlimited vision and dreams. You don't have to shed your doing identities to anchor to being identities. Ask yourself, "In what way do I want to show up in my roles?" Your answers should help you find a few different being anchors to consider.

I hope you are already feeling lighter as you have looked at the challenges that can weigh you down as you take off toward achieving impact. Remember: We each face these challenges in different ways and at different times. You may not need the work in every area right now, but when you need it, you know where to find the tools and how to build the skills to help you overcome these obstacles. If you have uncovered some stubborn areas that need more time and maybe even some outside help, focus on building your golden circle. The people in that circle can support you and offer new perspectives, strategies, and skills. I also hope the work here has diminished your uncomfortable feelings about past failure and you now see them as invested value to your future success. If you're not quite there, go back and run them through the Failure/Success Analysis Tool and then follow up with the FETBO Template for the past failure that is generating those lingering doubts. But if you're ready, let's continue the work of flight success!

TAKEAWAYS

- There are **four challenges on the journey to giving yourself permission to fly**: blame, self-trust, passivity, and identity.
  - **Blame** often manifests as judgmentalism. When you judge others, you assume your perspective is superior,

creating a self-serving bias that hinders success. To overcome this, use the FETBO Template, actively listen, seek diverse input, validate perspectives broadly, and surround yourself with trusted advisors who enrich, challenge, and refine your perspectives.

- **Self-trust** is often threatened by imposter syndrome when giving yourself permission to fly. This condition is the belief that you do not deserve or haven't actually earned your success. You can feel overwhelmed with automatic negative thoughts (ANTs), such as "I don't know what I'm doing" or "I'm not experienced enough." Use the FETBO Template to increase your awareness of these ANTs and replace them with more accurate thoughts (MATs).

- **Passivity** is often detrimental, though there are some forms of healthy passivity, including letting others show up how they want so you don't spend your energy trying to control the feelings and actions of others. There are times that call for purposeful passivity.

- **Identity** is an idea of who you are, which is anchored to your doing and/or being. Doing anchors hamper your connection to vision and dreams outside of your current roles while being anchors can be pulled in and dropped down to support new, unlimited vision and dreams. You don't have to shed your doing identities to anchor to being identities.

13

Fly Better

*The world needs dreamers and the world needs doers.
But above all, the world needs dreamers who do.*

—Sarah Ban Breathnach,
*Simple Abundance: A Daybook of
Comfort and Joy*

Flying in these pages means pursuing dreams, creating impact, and achieving success in your endeavors. Notice that the very first act of flight involves dreaming. So often, people relegate dreaming as something for small children or the creation of a bucket list, meaning things you want to do before you kick the bucket. Neither category is wrong, and while they both build our imagination and can be tapped to create motivation, they don't exactly fit our current purposes. Children's dreams are unhindered by the demands of reality because they don't sense the constraints of time, energy, and resources. Bucket lists are often centered on experiences a dreamer wants to have before they no longer can. But to fly, you need to have a vision of what that flight looks like beyond the parameters of the very young or those considering last-days desires. These dreams support the impact you want to create.

What happened to your ability to dream? I have found that there are a couple of reasons you can lose touch with not just your dreams but your *ability* to dream. As humans grow through the different phases of adulthood, the demands of daily life intensify. Your efficient brain wants to use its energy to keep you and those you are responsible for alive. On its own, the brain may shut down the conscious focus on things that do not immediately serve those functions. Additionally, you find that as you get older, priorities change and you let go of certain dreams from your younger days. This letting go of old dreams is absolutely appropriate. For example, do you still want to pursue the dream of having the shiny red five-speed when you have already acquired a lightweight road bike or a four-wheel drive hybrid for weekend adventures? No, but the *ability* to dream—that you want to nurture. Why is the ability to dream connected to permitting yourself to fly? Because without the imagination to picture what success could look like, you don't have anything pulling you forward except maybe the desire to achieve—but achieve what? You lose clarity when you can't dream about the impact you want to create. You need to retrain your brain to allocate energy for focus and, as you know, bossing your brain is a privilege and a responsibility that takes intention.

> **You lose clarity when you can't dream about the impact you want to create.**

PRACTICE DREAMING

- To kick off this retraining, write down thirty things you want. You may be thinking, "Well that's not so hard." But here is the trick: Make sure ten of those things are things you now have. I know, this feels a bit counterproductive, but you are providing evidence to your brain that you can want something and then have that thing. So, one-third of your list is actually things you have. Note that when I say "things," I don't mean only physical items. For example, a client and I recently worked through this exercise, and here are some of the things that comprised his list:

- I want to get a college education.
- I want to drive a hybrid car.
- I want to be a dad.
- I want to be a full-time chef.
- I want to create a garden that supplies vegetables year-round.
- I want to make a podcast and teach others how to grow and raise their own food.
- I want to be a runner.
- I want to compete in a bike race.
- I want to serve my community.

In this instance, my client was already a dad with a college education, and he was serving his community through volunteer work. Spend some time noticing the things you really want that you already have on your list. Put a check mark by those and sink into feelings of gratitude to God, yourself, parents, partners, or anyone who you feel contributed to making those things happen—just be sure to include yourself in this list. You worked toward those dreams; it wasn't just luck. Don't tuck this list away. Keep it visible by putting it on your phone, posting it on your bathroom mirror, or slipping it into your journal or paper calendar—some place you will see it regularly. Every time you look at it, lean into that feeling of gratitude. This list is not so much about noticing what you don't have yet but noticing what you *have* achieved and what you are still moving toward. We'll also refer back to this list later as we discuss impact.

The second practice to help remind our brains how to dream is to make a daily "power of three" practice by listing three things you want every morning. These can be things you put on your original list or something smaller or more in the moment. For example, I want my dog to stop eating socks, I want pizza for dinner, and I want to land a new client. It's not so much about the content of your desires but teaching your brain to notice your desires. This will be particularly helpful for those of you with passive tendencies. Once you've made that quick list, take thirty seconds or so (it will take longer at first, but you will get faster) to imagine that you have those things and let the feelings of having them fill you. As you imagine the feelings, use your emotional literacy to label them so that you can tap into your Library of Emotions to experience the physiological sensations of those feelings. In this way, you train your mind to get clear on what you want, exercise your imagination about how something that has not yet happened will be, and reward the practice with the physiological treats that come with desirable emotions.

My hiking friend performed a version of this in her evaluation of the prospect of taking the hike without her companion. She imagined dealing with the challenges of the hike with only herself to encourage and lead her own journey. She imagined hiking up the last incline and out to the other canyon rim alone. She imagined seeing her partner waiting for her at the top. This work helped her realize that doing it on her own was going to require more courage, add more risk, and provide more reward.

If permission to fail is about building muscles that can only be forged in the risk and reward of discovery, then permission to fly is about managing the currents of bold action, setting sights on a destination, and taking to the air—approach, adjust, and act.

If the idea of dreaming big is a struggle for you, I encourage you to feed that focus just a bit. To do that, read a book or watch a film about people who achieved great dreams. Fiction is fine, but something inspired by a true story will probably do a better job of providing evidence to your brain. Notice the emotions the person or protagonist experiences. Now notice the emotions of those around them. What beliefs pulled them through the challenges of pursuing that dream? Keep immersing yourself in these stories to support the idea that big dreams can be achieved.

> A few stories I recommend: *Hidden Figures, Apollo 13, Cool Runnings, Hoosiers, Boys in the Boat, The Devil Wears Prada,* and *Lessons in Chemistry*

These two exercises are helping activate muscles that support dreaming. Now that you've practiced flexing that muscle, let's do the work of building a list of flight dreams.

STAGES OF FLIGHT DREAMS

Maybe the work of training your brain to tune in to your dream power has felt foreign, or maybe you are one of the rare few who has never unintentionally or intentionally distanced yourself from your dreams. But studies have found an interesting pattern in people's relationship with dreams that is influenced by age and stage of life. These studies reveal that as you age, your attitudes toward dreams change. In your younger years, you set goals to help you achieve your dreams. Then in middle age, some of those dreams are achieved and some are put aside in order to maintain the dreams you have achieved. Finally, in older age, you notice that most of your goals revolve around protecting from or at least slowing down the loss of those things you worked so hard to achieve. In this stage, you often grieve the dreams you feel there is no longer time to pursue.[1]

As I was thinking about these studies and how I wanted to share this information, I reflected on a family trip and noticed that we take some interesting family walks when we're away together. I don't mean to come across as morbid, but as a family we enjoy taking in historic graveyards, imagining the lives of those whose remains are laid to rest there; these places are peaceful, often beautiful, and give perspective to each breath we take. On this particular trip, we took a stroll through a very old cemetery in Washington, DC. It is not far from where we usually stay when we visit DC, and we had walked past it a number of times while doing errands on busy Wisconsin Avenue. Passing through those gates just a few steps off the crowded multi-lane road, we entered a sacred place where the stories of people who had dreams centuries ago are commemorated. What did those people want to accomplish during that small dash between the year they were born and the time that they left this Earth? Like I said, perspective.

Wherever you fall on the spectrum of age, I hope as you read about this research on age and dreaming, you've identified where you are. I work with a number of older adults about legacy thinking, and I have shared this research with some of my clients. Most of the time, they identify as no longer pursuing dreams they held at a younger age and sometimes not pursuing any dreams at all. For them, this work can bring up a number of emotions, just as it may for you. However, those clients learn to identify an emotion, understand the message, and work to create goals that honor the values that feel threatened, no matter how much energy, time, or money they may have.

I'm wondering what feelings show up for you when reading about this research—maybe sadness, joy, disappointment, or even excitement? Do the work of labeling those feelings and look for the messages. You now know how to process and appreciate those feelings.

I share that study with you to create awareness of the typical correlative attitude between age and dreams. Now that you know, you can see those tendencies and change them. What does this have to do with permission to fly? No matter your age, you need dreams to help you get clarity of destination and motivation to lift your flight off the ground. To approach this permission and repair your flight mechanism, you must reconnect with dreams, prioritize them, and strategize success. The muscles you have built in the last two sections of the book will support you in these same steps to take flight.

LEVERAGE THE POWER OF DREAMING

I once worked with a client we'll call Mike, whose spouse passed away when his two daughters were very young. He worked hard to be an involved parent and have a very successful career to provide for his family. Now that his daughters were grown, he was struggling to find his focus. His tendency was to keep up his level of involvement in his daughters' lives, but they were sending him strong messages that they could and wanted to make their own decisions without his input, which they felt was overbearing.

One of the ways we worked to shift his focus was by helping Mike reconnect with his dreaming skills. For so long, his focus was on helping his children connect with their dreams, but he had forgotten how to dream for himself. Sharing with Mike the information about how people treat dreaming in different seasons helped him normalize his behavior and recognize that he could change. Mike categorized himself as being in the middle-age range of trying to maintain the dreams he had already achieved rather than pursuing new or old unachieved dreams, and this awareness prepared him to do the work of finding what he now wanted to fly toward.

Based on the distance you feel from your dreams, you can choose how in-depth you want to take this work, because reconnecting is work that takes intention and energy. Mike felt very far from a time when he dreamed for himself. In fact, he had the mindset that dreaming for himself was actually selfish. How do you feel about dreaming? Do you think of it as something you used to do? In your mind, do you feel that dreaming is only for the young? That it somehow implies selfishness or immaturity? Or is it something you avoid to prevent disappointment? It's okay if these are your thoughts, but know that without dreaming, you are limiting the way you create impact in this world. Maybe that is fine with you, but I'm guessing that since you are currently reading a book about giving yourself permission to feel, fail, and fly, you actually have a desire to fly further and higher than you already are. There is no judgment in these pages—if you have worked through the first two parts of the book and don't feel like you are in a season when you need or want to fly to new or different heights, that is absolutely okay. I encourage you to release any thoughts of self-judgment as well. We've already done quite a bit of work about self-compassion, so I'll leave it with a simple encouragement to reflect on and honor the work of your current season with kindness.

So, how you can reconnect with your dreams? Even if you still remember your previous dreams, they may have changed a bit as you have entered new seasons of life. Similar to Mike's story, in your own life, each season requires a different focus and that means how you look at and prioritize your dreams changes as well. But you will not be relegating your efforts to protecting what you have already achieved.

Because I know saying, "Write down all your dreams" can cause a deer-in-the-headlights sort of response, I like to offer my clients categories to help narrow down the field of dreams. I want to make sure you are clear about what I mean by dreams. If you and I were in coaching session together, I would ask you to provide a definition about what a dream means to you. For the purposes of this book, I propose we agree that a dream is something you imagine, envision, and want very much to do, be, or have. This is an unfolding process.

Imagine a piece of paper crumpled up tightly. Depending on the type of paper it is, it may unfold at a different pace, and it may even need a little assistance to fully open up. Unfolding your dreams may take a bit of time and energy, especially if you haven't given yourself space to explore this lately. Take a deep breath, let your shoulders relax, and enjoy this process. There are no wrong answers. These are your dreams. For the first part of this work, resist the tendency to self-edit. Resistance may show up in the form of practicalities or other constraints. Recognize that dreaming means change, and our brains resist anything that moves it out of efficient stasis. Thank it for trying to keep you safe and assure your brain that you are excited about and safe with this effort. We'll do the work of making these dreams into goals later, but for now, just dream with me.

For each category, make a quick list of dream ideas. I do recommend that you write these down rather than type them. Studies show that a different part of your creative brain is activated when you handwrite, and you want those creative juices flowing. You may want a page per category to give space for future dreams as well. However, getting them articulated is the most important thing, so if you don't have pen and paper, "needs must."

Consider these categories:

- **Relationships**—What kind of friendship/romantic dreams make your heart quicken?
- **Financial**—What kind of monetary dreams do you long for?
- **Educational**—What would you love to learn?
- **Spiritual**—What would support your ideal spiritual growth?
- **Hobbies**—What interests would you love to have time to pursue?
- **Service**—In what ways would you enjoy pouring into others?
- **Legacy**—What would you like to be remembered for?

THE SO METHOD

○ Great work on loosening your mind and generating dreams for each area. Now, let's build a little more clarity about the impact achieving those dreams could create. To do this, we'll be using an approach called The "So" Method. Don't worry—this should feel like a good stretch. Be sure to notice the emotions that show up as you unpack the why behind your dreams. For each category, choose one dream that feels the most important right now. This is not a limitation but a prioritization. All your dreams are important, but for now, focus on one per category.

Now that you have prioritized, take one of your priority dreams and finish this statement:

"I want to _____
(your dream)

so that I can _____."
(what achieving that dream will allow you to do)

Example: *"I want to finish my degree so that I can get a raise."*

Great! Now we'll repeat—kind of. Fill in this next sentence:

"I want to _____
(your previous dream achievement statement)

so that I can _____."
(what that achievement will create)

Example: *"I want to get a raise so that I can start a college savings account for my children."*

Now do the last step again but fill in your most recent "so that I can" achievement statement:

> **Example:** *"I want to start a college savings account so that I can <u>show my kids through my example and my provision that education is valuable.</u>"*

As you finish the third "so" statement, you will probably feel a tug on your emotions. Be sure to process as I know you know how to do. What values are your emotions revealing to you through this dream? You can stop at one dream or work through this exercise with your priority dream from each category.

This is ongoing work. For each of these dreams—and any new ones you decide to add later—you can move toward achievement, not all of them at once, but let them inspire you just as much as your little child self was inspired to be a train engineer rock star. You will soon leverage the Failure/Success Analysis Tool to set strategic goals to move toward your dreams, but return to this list of flight dreams anytime you need a little inspiration.

Let's circle back to Mike and how his dreams look through this exercise.

- **Relationships:** Mike relied on his daughters' activities to provide him social connections while they were growing up—the volleyball parents, the other parents who volunteered to build sets for the theater group, etc. Now he realized he needs to look at what kind of relationships he wants to pursue on his own. He wants to make some friends around his own interests, which are hiking and photography. He also had a goal to build a romantic relationship, but he had not made space in his life to date since his wife died more than a decade ago.

- **Financial:** Mike has created a lot of success in his career that translates into financial comfort, but he wants to actually use some of that to pursue his hobbies while saving to leave his daughters and eventually grandchildren comfortable as well.

- **Educational:** Mike wanted to learn more about photography. He was self-taught but a photographer that he admires offers a retreat to teach techniques that inspire Mike.

- **Spiritual:** Mike felt he has neglected his spiritual growth and dreamed of feeling spiritually connected and peaceful.

- **Hobbies**: Mike dreamed of hiking internationally as well as capturing amazing photographs of his travels.

- **Service**: Mike wanted to serve the homeless in his community.

- **Legacy:** Mike wanted to be remembered as a kind provider and supporter of his family, friends, and community.

The next step for Mike was to apply The So Method you walked through earlier. I won't go over his answers here, but I will say that when Mike connected his dreams to his whys, it was very evident that there was nothing selfish about them.

Remember how we talked about dreams and a bucket list? Bucket items often do have an element of selfishness in them. I believe that once you apply The So Method, you, like Mike, will discover that your reasons for these dreams are deeper than just what you get out of it. Every action you take produces some kind of effect, and they don't exist in a vacuum where that effect is only experienced by you, the one who took action. Most often, another life or environment is also affected by your actions. I want you to notice the impact of the results you create.

Have you ever been to an aquarium show where there were signs posted around seats closest to the tank: "Get ready to get wet! You're in the splash zone!" I want you to think about the "splash zone" of achieving your dreams. Who will be impacted by the dreams you achieve? They fall into the impact zone. I want you to first do the following exercise using items on the list you already generated of thirty things that you want. Specifically, use the things on that list that you want and already have.

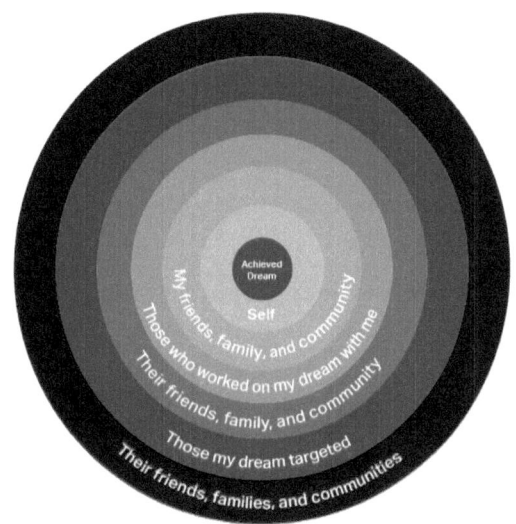

Image 13.1: Dream Impact Zone

Think about the item you've chosen from your list. Using the aforementioned impact zone graphic as a model, list the impact achieving that desire created. This doesn't have to be an exhaustive list, but start connecting with the collateral benefit of your dreams.

On my list, I have "Be a mom." For this exercise, "Be a mom" goes in the center circle. Then in the next circle going outward, I can place me, then my husband, my girls, my parents, my in-laws, my grandparents, my friends, and their families. I chuckle when I think of those who worked on my dream of motherhood, because it is actually more than just my spouse—it also includes the adoption agency, the infertility doctors and nurses, the friends who encouraged me on my parenting journey, my girls' teachers, and the community where we parent. The next circle would be my daughters' friends, their communities . . . and the circles continue to ripple out. The impact zone is infinite. So, is it actually selfish to dream or selfish *not* to dream? I hope you've noticed that impactful dreams are not me-centric—they are dream-centric.

For dreams to be most impactful, they must be meaningful. This exercise helps you grasp just how meaningful your dreams are. Once you have identified the impact zone for a dream you have already achieved, move on to a different dream from The So Method exercise. As you fill out the circles, notice the emotions that show up. Incredulity? Awe? Surprise? Love? These feelings support the driving power of achieving impactful dreams. Great work getting clear on your dreams and expanding awareness about the impact of those dreams.

CRUCIAL FLIGHT VISIBILITY

My family and I live in a large metro area that has an international airport. Most of our news weather reports are based on what is happening at the airport. Almost daily, we get a visibility report because, when you think about it, for flight safety and success, visibility plays a crucial role. It turns out that visibility plays an important role in your flight success as well.

Think about this statement: "What we pay attention to, we become." When you pay attention to something, that means you're looking at it. When my girls were learning to drive, in all my parental wisdom, which they so enjoyed, I used to compel them to scan their surroundings with their eyes but always keep their focus on the road, not the scenery or a cute dog or person on the sidewalk because, when driving, you follow your focus. This applies to flying as well.

> **What you focus on, you become.**

To make this personal: What you focus on, you become. This isn't just a tendency. In fact, science shows that humans are created with equipment that manifests this behavior. What you focus on consistently changes the shape of your brain. Neuroscientists Eleanor Maguire and Katherine Woollett performed a five-year study of London cab drivers that confirms this. Maguire and Woollett measured portions of the brains as well as the mental aptitude of seventy-nine aspiring cabbies and a control group of thirty-one people of similar age, education, and intelligence. To train as London cabbies, applicants had to pass a Knowledge of London test, which required four years of studying London traffic, routes, and places of interest. At the beginning of the study, all participants had similar-sized hippocampi (the part of the brain involved in forming, storing, and processing memory) as well as similar performance on mental memory tests. At the end of the four-and-a-half-year study, thirty-nine of the seventy-nine cabbie applicants succeeded in passing the test. All of the study's participants (those who passed, failed, and the control group of non-applicants) repeated the pre-study evaluations. Those who had passed the Knowledge of London test performed significantly better on the mental testing than the other participants and better than they themselves had performed four years earlier. Additionally, MRIs showed that their hippocampi had physically increased in size.[2] What you focus on consistently changes your brain, and your brain development changes who you become. This will happen whether you are guiding your focus or letting your attention be pulled along by whatever current you find yourself in. Those who want to fly must choose to focus on thoughts, behaviors, and people that support flight. So how does this apply to visibility?

Make what you want to give attention to as visible as possible. Remember: Visibility is crucial to flight. To be honest, life provides many things that pull for your attention. The good news is that you are equipped to handle the constant input that life provides. This equipment is the reticular activating system (RAS). The RAS is a network of neurons in the brain stem that is responsible for a number of functions like alertness, attention, and consciousness. It is built to filter out a good portion of the data your senses are taking in to keep your brain from becoming overwhelmed. It is like a gatekeeper in that only the things your conscious mind gives importance to get in.

Pay attention here: The RAS filters what you think about, whether it is good for you or not. For example, you buy a pair of bright purple boots that you love. They feel uniquely you when you purchase them. Suddenly, it feels like many of the people you see are now wearing purple boots. What happened? Did everyone everywhere wake up to the beauty of purple boots? Nope, you did—or more accurately, your RAS did. Because you gave focus to purple boots, your RAS started allowing all the instances of purple boots through to your conscious awareness. You can see how the RAS works to support cognitive bias where you find what you are searching for, but also see that you can put the RAS to intentional work by choosing what you want to get through its filter.[3]

So how do you do that? You've already accomplished the first steps by generating a list of dreams, focusing on the deeper reasons for those dreams, and creating awareness of the exponential impact achieving those dreams creates. Next is making the dreams you have been crafting visible by creating visibility boards. Work past any negative associations you have with the term "vision board" and think about how interior designers, architects, business planners, landscapers, writers, dentists, cake artists, and other professionals all recognize the value of creating a visual representation of something that does not yet exist. You may find it helpful to call it a "flight visibility board." Have fun with this. You can work on a board for each dream category or make a collage of your most important dreams. Gather magazines, print photos from online, and create headings. Make it free-form or very structured and symmetrical, but create it.

My daughter once shared with me about the joy she found in making Pinterest vision boards. It is really fun because it is so easy, and your input sources are literally anything online. However, if you choose to use that medium for your visibility board, consider printing out the elements so you do not have to rely on technology to view it. Remember that you want to make these dreams as visible as possible to help your RAS to support your flight. A word of warning: Just making the board is helpful but to really train your RAS, you will need to keep it visible. Hang your board(s) someplace you will see it daily. Take a photo of your board and make it your lock screen on your phone. You get the idea: Keep this visibility board highly visible. After all, a flight attempting to take off in low visibility will not leave the ground.

Reconnecting with your dreaming skills and leveraging the power of focus can support your flight mindset. Take your time to process and build up these skills. When you're ready, move on to learn about how you actually achieve liftoff!

TAKEAWAYS

- **A dream is something you imagine, envision, and want very much to do, be, or have.** The ability *to dream* is a skill that comes naturally in childhood, but which you must nurture consciously in adult life. Without the imagination to picture what success could look like, you don't have anything pulling you forward except maybe the desire to achieve. You lose clarity when you can't dream about the impact you want to create, so you must retrain your brain.

- **Practice dreaming** by writing out a list of what you want in different areas of your life (relationships, financial, educational, spiritual, hobbies, service, legacy), including some things you already have. Keep this list visible and practice gratitude for the things you've already acquired.

- **Make a daily power of three practice** by listing three things you want every morning. Imagine that you have those things and let the feelings of having them fill you. When you imagine the feelings, use your emotional literacy to label them so that you can tap into your Library of Emotions to experience the physiological sensations of those feelings.

- **Dreams change during the course of your life.** In your younger years, you set goals to help you achieve your dreams. Then in middle age, some of those dreams are achieved and some are put aside in order to maintain the dreams you have achieved. Finally, in older age, you notice that most of your goals revolve around protecting from or at least slowing down the loss of those things you worked so hard to achieve. Awareness of where you fall on this spectrum will help you clarify your destination and the direction of your journey.

- **Reconnecting with your dreams may take a bit of time and energy**, especially if you haven't given yourself space to explore this lately. For the first part of this work, resist the tendency to self-edit. There are no wrong answers. These are your dreams. Build more clarity about the impact achieving your dreams could create using the "so method."

- **Create awareness of the exponential impact of achieving your dreams** by imagining the positive ripple effect your success would create for those around you—friends, family, and the greater community.

- **What you focus on, you become.** Make what you want to give attention to as visible as possible. Create a "flight visibility board" to help keep your eye on your goals.

14

Flight Plan for Liftoff

Once, as I sat onboard a packed 747 at the gate ready to taxi for takeoff, I was given reason to consider flight plans. The reason was the pilot announcing that the tower had delayed our flight because air traffic control didn't like our current flight plan. After an hour and a half of us waiting on the plane while the new flight plan was negotiated, the tower was comfortable enough to let us take off. The incident made me a curious about flight plans, and as a curious person does (and because I had an hour and a half to fiddle on my phone), I did some searching. An article from the Aircraft Performance Group explained that a flight plan is filed to keep data updated and clarify communication for all stakeholders with safety in the air and on the ground a priority.[1] What was really interesting to me, though, was this statement in the article about what determines the flight plan: "To avoid air traffic incidents, pilots use various 'rules' based on their intended type of flying." The writer went on to explain that different kinds of flights have different rules for their flight plans. Similarly, as you create a plan for your success, you have to consider your dreams, your beliefs, your rules, and your goals.

MAKING YOUR FLIGHT PLAN

Start by creating a flight plan based on the dreams you have generated and made visible. Do this by transforming those dreams into intentions and gaining pre-sight to inform your planning. Once again, using a familiar tool in a different way can yield fresh results. In this case, you're repurposing the Failure/Success Analysis Tool not to process an after-action review but to apply critical thinking to your dream intentions. To use this tool in this instance, choose one of your priority dreams to fill the intention line. As you do so, recognize the value of the tools you are learning: Dreams are rarely realized unintentionally. A few people do win the lottery, but, statistically speaking, most do not. Intentions are important and clarity of intentions will make sure you are heading in your desired direction. Thinking back to my friend's Grand Canyon hike, planning, preparing, and packing for the trip would not have been a useful investment of her energy, time, or money if she had not intended to take the journey.

Just as I noted earlier about dreams, intentions are unlimited. However, the most powerful intentions are aligned with your dreams, goals, passions, and values. I've chosen a few examples of intentions to focus on as we go on: writing a book, getting a promotion, and improving social interactions. Let's see what this looks like for you by building on what you did in the previous chapter. Follow these steps:

- Once you've chosen a dream and clarified your intention from that dream, spend some time visualizing a successful outcome for your intention. Don't rush this step. It may seem obvious at first but think about what would express your success.

- Now to the counterpart: What would failure to implement your intention look like? Again, spend time noticing the outward signals of failure in this intention.

- Now that you are clear on what both success and failure look like, let's get clear on the actions that create those outcomes.

What actions would make your vision of success possible?
What actions would make your vision of failure probable?

INTENTION: (FILL IN THE BLANK)

What does success look like?	What choices/actions would make success possible?
What does failure look like?	What choices/actions would make failure probable?

Once you've completed your analysis, answer a few debrief questions to tap into the pre-sight of your results:

- What of your current systems, habits, and actions align with the success actions in your analysis?
- What of your current systems, habits, and actions align with the failure actions in your analysis?

- What will you need to give up in order to take on the actions that would make success possible?
- If you met your future self on the day you successfully achieve this intention, what would your future self say?
  Complete the sentence: "I'm so grateful to my past self for _____."
  (fill in the blank)

Now that you have walked through the process, have a look at a few examples of the tool in action.

INTENTION: FINISH MY BOOK DRAFT IN THREE WEEKS

What does success look like?	What choices/actions would make success possible?
• Full draft done—all three sections • Waiting for edits from manuscript editor • Positive advance reader feedback • Feel good about potential impact of work	• Writing on a regular schedule • Prioritizing the work • Setting ambitious writing milestones • Giving the manuscript to pre-readers and requesting feedback • Seeking out volunteers to test the models
What does failure look like?	What choices/actions would make failure probably?
• No work done on book • Frustration and lack of confidence • Letting my editor down • No impact with my work	• Writing only when I feel like it • Focusing on other goals • Not sharing my work

Here's another example, using the idea of seeking a promotion at work:

INTENTION: GET PROMOTED AT WORK

What does success look like?
- Change my role in three months
- Make more money
- Have more responsibility
- Get positive feedback from my peers and supervisor

What choices/actions would make success possible?
- Ask for a mentor
- Find out promotion requirements
- Ask for cross-training/development opportunities
- Show up as a valuable team member

What does failure look like?
- Poor feedback from my peers and supervisors
- Stay in my same role
- Make the same salary
- Have the same responsibility

What choices/actions would make failure probably?
- Ignore past feedback I was offered
- Don't seek mentorship
- Stay unaware of steps to promotion
- Do not request extra training
- Don't show up consistently for work
- Have a just-get-by attitude

And here's an example for expanding one's social interactions:

INTENTION: EXPAND MY SOCIAL INTERACTIONS

What does success look like?
- Fewer full days alone
- Several new friends who I see a couple of times a month
- One close friend who I see weekly

What choices/actions would make success possible?
- Join a common interest group—a painting class, museum volunteering, walking club
- Invite someone to meet each week for lunch, coffee, or a walk
- Have an open attitude about meeting new people; see everyone as valuable
- Communicate with a friend every day

What does failure look like?
- Seven days a week with no social gatherings
- Feeling lonely
- Experiencing frustration when doing solo activities

What choices/actions would make failure probably?
- Stay at home and binge watch TV shows
- Wait and hope to be invited out
- Judge everyone
- Avoid answering emails and texts, so I don't have to choose between different options

Now that you are familiar with this application, let's jump into a case study. Like my client in this case, you may find dissonance between what you are currently doing and your dream intention. Resist the urge to indulge in either-or thinking. Notice how working through the tool a couple of times helps you generate more inclusive strategies. Once we've completed the Failure/Success Analysis, you'll have what you need to set goals and take action to achieve flight.

AVOIDING EITHER-OR THINKING

One client, Connie, a creative in her late twenties, was working a day job and had recently been promoted to a management position in the marketing department. However, her heart sang when she was telling stories through photography. While she did some of that in her work, she didn't get to choose what stories she told, and she didn't love managing others. When she came to me for help, she was frustrated about spending so much of her time doing work that felt meaningless and tired of trying to manage and train new team members, yet she was scared of quitting and losing the steady income both she and her partner depended upon.

Over the course of our work, Connie strengthened her self-management and her management of others. Using many of the tools shared here, Connie realized she could work toward the vision of being a full-time artist while still paying her bills with her marketing role. First, we used the Failure/Success Tool to gain pre-sight with the intention "I want to do meaningful work." Then we did it again with the intention "I want to provide for me and my partner and while they are finishing their education." You can see in the following models that it feels as if there is a tension between the two. But here is the thing: In seeking clarity, you can unconsciously lock into an either-or belief pattern. This is often easier and requires less mental energy, so it feels good to your always efficiency-seeking brain. But in giving yourself permission to boss your brain to create flight, you can leverage your superpower of holding multiple feelings and seemingly diverse intentions at the same time. Look at how this worked out for Connie.

It's important that when you look at these examples, you don't get sucked into judgmentalism. These examples may not reflect how you would complete your Failure/Success Analysis, but that is not the point. The goal here is not to address a specific circumstance in a prescribed way but to equip yourself to build confidence in approaching, adjusting to, and acting in any circumstance to create your desired impact. By now, you know how to notice when judgmentalism rears up and you know how to refocus. Be sure to apply those skills here or you will miss the usefulness of the analysis itself.

Model 1 for Connie follows, presented as a simple list. You can use the graphic I provided or just jot these ideas down on paper. The important thing is that you engage with the process.

INTENTION: I WANT TO DO MEANINGFUL PHOTOGRAPHY WORK.

Success

- I spend my time on projects I choose.
- I choose how to tell the story of each project.
- My work is exciting to me and all who encounter it.
- I make money on my chosen projects.
- I pay my bills from meaningful work.
- I look forward to my work daily.

Actions that support success

- Devoting all of my time to chosen projects.
- Creating an editing studio at home.
- Making a full portfolio that showcases my skills and art.
- Seeking an artist's agent.
- Seeking great stories to tell.

Failure
- I keep working fifty hours a week in a marketing job.
- I don't choose my clients.
- I am bored and do subpar work.
- I feel sad, discouraged.
- I have no portfolio and no work to showcase my skills and art.
- I resent my partner for relying on my income.

Actions that support failure
- Keep my head down at work and try to power through my boredom.
- Spend my nonwork time on cleaning, shopping, and food prep to keep my home running smoothly.
- Look for ways to distract from my sadness.
- Don't look for support from anyone else to pursue my dreams.
- Try to focus on marketing to improve my work.

And here's Model 2 for Connie:

INTENTION: PAY MY BILLS WITH A MARKETING JOB.

Success
- I have enough money to pay bills, save for a house, and support my partner in finishing their education.
- I start enjoying my work and am energized by it.
- I improve my management skills.
- I get a raise.

Actions that support success

- I network with other marketing professionals for support.
- I ask for manager development at work.
- I seek a marketing mentor.
- I pursue the next step in my marketing career.
- I ask for a raise.
- I focus each day on creating value for my bosses.
- Create work/life balance.

Failure

- I do poor work and don't manage people well.
- I get fired or demoted.
- I have to drag myself out of bed each morning.
- I leave my partner/my partner leaves me.
- I am no longer an artist.

Actions that support failure

- Keep focusing on my frustration
- Try to stay off my boss's radar and avoid interaction with her
- Work by myself and limit interaction with those I manage
- Call in sick to work when I can't get myself out of bed
- Spend more time at work and less at home

I hope you notice, as Connie did, that when these two pre-sight models are side by side, there is tension between the intentions. And we know that truth is in the tension. Connie was approaching her circumstance with binary thinking—meaning something is all good or all bad. She could only do meaningful work if she gave all of her time to her art, and she could only meet her financial goals if she gave all of her energy to her marketing job.

There is value in both of these pre-sights. Learning happened around each intention and that learning expanded when we put them together. When Connie answered the pre-sight debrief questions, she learned that working toward the time where she could fully focus on her art created meaning and gave her energy. She needed to change some habits to accommodate goals that addressed both intentions. She set those goals based on a combination of actions from the two different intention analyses. It also helped Connie to notice her identity markers were also victims of her either-or thinking; she recognized "artist" was a *doing* identifier where "artistic" identified a way of *being*. She noticed actions she could take in small steps to feed her artistic identity, and her brain had enough evidence to confirm this identity. She realized she didn't have to work full time in art to consider herself artistic. She could anchor this identifier with both her marketing job and her photography.

This exercise of mental contrasting is helpful for all the reasons we've already discussed, but let's look at what you can do to make this information even more impactful by making it the foundation of your goals.

Before you move ahead with this process, make sure you have answered the pre-sight debrief questions. With that done, I recommend working with quarterly goals. You can have a twelve-month goal, but to create motivating momentum, break that larger goal into three-month chunks. With the model you just completed, ask yourself if your vision of success could be accomplished in three months or, with that vision in mind, ask yourself what successfully moving toward it would look like given three months' time. Look at the actions for the success portion of the pre-sight Failure/Success Analysis that you just completed. What of those actions could you implement in the next three months? When you worked through the pre-sight debrief questions, you may have discovered new actions to support success such as changing a habit or adopting a new system. These can be incorporated in your goals.

SMART GOALS

- Using your updated success action list, prioritize those actions and make the top one a SMART Goal.[2] In case you are not familiar with SMART Goals, it is an acronym first developed by George T. Doran, a management consultant, in 1981, for use in helping managers clarify department goals. However, Doran's system was so effective that it has since been expanded for individual goalsetting. Doran's original acronym guided managers to craft goals that are **S**pecific, **M**easurable, **A**chievable, **R**ealistic, and **T**angible. In more modern-day use, the T now stands for Timebound. Along with the acronym, Doran listed some questions to help users work through his model. "Let me suggest therefore, that when it comes to writing effective objectives, corporate officers, managers, and supervisors just have to think of the acronym SMART. Ideally speaking, each corporate, department, and section objective should be: [SMART]," he said.

You also can leverage Doran's creation to help you set effective goals for your flight plan. These goals are another facet of making your invisible dreams visible. Record each of these elements on a card or piece of paper. Using one of the actions from your pre-sight Failure/Success Analysis create a SMART Goal. (You can put several actions together in one goal if they seem like related steps to the same thing.) You may ask, why isn't my intention my goal? Your intention is still there, and you are moving toward it, but it can be overwhelming to plot all the steps needed to get there and try to achieve it in one giant leap. If you make just one of the steps a goal, you will see your progress, feel accomplished, build momentum, and get a better sense of the impact of your intention. Additionally, I want to support the idea that your goals are not destinations but mile markers along your journey. Your action of working toward this goal will actually bring greater clarity to your intention. The action permission principle always brings clarity. Don't worry—we'll walk through a few questions to help you clarify every element of your SMART Goal.

- **Specific:** What do you want to achieve? Be as detailed about this as you can.
- **Measurable:** What signs or metrics will indicate to you that you are succeeding at this goal? This is often one of the more challenging aspects for my clients when working on goals.
- **Achievable:** How will you achieve this? Think: "I will achieve this by (fill in action)." If you struggle, ask someone to help you brainstorm actions that would move you closer to achieving this goal. If you're still struggling to fill out this line, you may need to shift your goal.
- **Relevant:** This is just a check in because this goal should already have passed the test of relevance in your pre-sight Failure/Success Analysis. It should be related to supporting your intention.
- **Timebound:** This is basically a deadline. By when will this be achieved? I recommend allotting yourself no more than three months (one quarter). If your goal doesn't fit in that timeline, break it down into smaller steps.

I'd like you to recall that setting these goals supports flight in a number of ways, but it is a crucial element of training your RAS. These goals need to be visible—I'm talking about reading them several times a day if possible. I also ask that you intentionally reflect on them.

Here's what I mean: If you tape this card to your bathroom mirror, it is visible, but just like that vintage jar of my dad's old marbles gave me so much joy when I first put it on display, now after it has been there a few weeks, you don't really notice it unless you intentionally look. I want you to intentionally look at these SMART Goals. A photo of these as the lock screen on your phone would be a powerful prompt, or consider paperclipping this card inside your daily calendar. Wherever you post it, make sure you read it daily.

Here are a few examples of SMART Goals:

SMART GOAL EXAMPLE 1 ─────────────
S—Write on a regular schedule.
M—I will record on my calendar each day I achieve my goal of writing and plan to achieve it at least five days per week.
A—I will achieve this by blocking time on both my client and student calendars, enlisting the support of my family for no interruptions, and asking my writers' group to hold me accountable.
R—This is relevant to support my intention of finishing my book in three months.
T—I will achieve a regular writing schedule in six weeks.

SMART GOAL EXAMPLE 2 ─────────────
S—Ask for a mentor at work.
M—Every Friday, I will check in to make sure I have completed one of my achievable steps.
A—I will do this by researching how my employer connects mentees and mentors. I will look up possible mentors on LinkedIn. I will write out what I hope to gain from and bring to a mentor relationship.
R—This is relevant to support my intention of a promotion at work.
T—I will achieve asking for a mentor by the end of four weeks.

SMART GOAL EXAMPLE 3

S—Join a common interest group.

M—By Sunday of the first week, I will have generated my list. By Sunday of the second week, I have explored each group. By the Sunday of the third week, I will have tried each group. By Sunday of the fourth week, I will have joined at least one group.

A—I will achieve this by generating a list of local volunteer and hobby groups. I will narrow the group to four and research each of those. I will go and try out each group. I will choose at least one group to join.

R—This is relevant to support my intention of expanding my social circle.

T—I will achieve joining a common interest group by the end of four weeks.

SMART GOAL EXAMPLE 4

S—Develop my emotional labeling skills.

M—I will measure my development by keeping a daily journal of how many times I labeled my emotions during the day. I will reflect on the week's journal entries each Sunday evening to notice how I'm doing and how specifically I am labeling. I will know I am successful when I automatically notice and label every strong emotion.

A—I will achieve this by using the Feelings Wheel to get more specific and setting alarms throughout the day to remind me to check in and practice labeling.

R—This is relevant because I am permitting myself to do this work to support feelings fitness that will help me to partner with my emotions to create the impact I want with my time, energy, and focus.

T—I want to be almost automatic at labeling all emotions by the end of the quarter.

If, in one of your daily goal readings, you notice that by your measurement metric, you are not moving toward achievement, adjust! Use your FETBO Template and put the goal in the outcome line. What do you need to feel, think, and do to achieve this goal? If this doesn't create new awareness for you, change the outcome, which means changing your goal. What could you achieve that will keep you moving toward your intention? Reset your SMART Goal and then take action. Nothing is written in stone. This is why one of the principles of permission is adjust. This permission gives us the ability to feel fit, fail effectively, and fly impactfully.

TAKEAWAYS

- As you **create a "flight plan" for your success**, you have to consider your dreams, your beliefs, your rules, and your goals. Repurpose the **Failure/Success Analysis Tool**, not to process an after-action review, but to apply critical thinking to your dream intentions to give yourself pre-sight into achieving them.

- **Intentions are important** and clarity of intentions will ensure you are heading in your desired direction. Spend some time visualizing a successful outcome for your intention. Also consider what outward signals of failure in this intention would look like.

- **Resist the urge to indulge in either-or thinking.** Working through the Failure/Success Analysis Tool a couple of times helps generate more inclusive strategies. The goal is not to address a specific circumstance in a prescribed way but to equip yourself to build confidence in approaching, adjusting to, and acting in any circumstance to create your desired impact.

- **Use SMART Goals** (goals that are Specific, Measurable, Achievable, Relevant, and Tangible/Timebound) to help you set effective markers of progress for your flight plan. Using one of the actions from your pre-sight Failure/Success Analysis, create a SMART Goal. Your action of working toward this goal will bring greater clarity to your intention.

15

Practicing the Principles of Flying

You should now be taking to the air with your clarified and goal-aligned actions in sight. Now let's shift gears just a little and look at another way to support your flight work. The next flight support may feel like a bit of a regression in your efforts. However, I wanted you to first formulate your route and the steps to move forward so that you can better notice any resistance or drag as you attempt flight. Our next work will help clarify why you might be frustrated and feeling resistance to taking action on those goals. In the previous chapter, I mentioned how important rules are to formulating a flight plan. Now turn your attention to the relationship between beliefs and rules and the system you create around that relationship. To put this in the context of our flight metaphor, you can have the best ideas for a flight plan, the most skilled pilots, fuel tanks filled to the brim, but if your navigation system is not functioning, you will not have a successful flight.

> **Beliefs and rules compose a system that can support or work against your goals.**

To be clear, for our purposes in these pages, a belief is a basic conviction or opinion that something is true in the form of repeated thought, and a rule is behavior that is or is not acceptable according to your beliefs. Based on their beliefs, humans create rules about how they will or will not act. This can sometimes create tension between a goal and an underlying belief. In other words, beliefs and rules compose a system that can support or work against your goals. For example, say you have a goal of never getting a speeding ticket. If you believe speed limits are immutable laws and the key to driving survival, your rule will be to never exceed a posted speed limit, and that supports your goal of not getting a ticket for speeding. However, if you believe speed limits are guidelines that are key for a beginner driver's safety, your rule may be that how fast you drive is determined by how much driving experience you have. This belief increases your odds of speeding as an experienced driver and works against your goal of not getting a speeding ticket. If your goals are not supported by your beliefs, you will struggle to take actions to achieve those goals.

Before you work to align your beliefs and your goals, I want to make sure we've unpacked how powerful beliefs and rules can be. One way this has shown up in my life was when, in order to deal with a difficult season of health issues, I created "rules" that I became more and more adherent to as my struggles dragged on. I don't mean that I sat down and wrote out a list of rules. Rather, I constructed them as I went, based on beliefs I formed while trying to make sense of my illness. A steady stream of new physical symptoms, testing, and treatments kept popping up, and I often felt like a duck in a shooting gallery game that turns anytime a new shot is fired. Every time a setback came, I would think, *Well I must not eat that food, go to this place, or do this specific task or I'll get sick again.* To some extent, everyone lives by self-imposed rules based on beliefs that help them make sense of the world. For me, it was trying to make sense of each new symptom or episode. For you, your sense-making brain is trying to figure out what beliefs will address or explain your challenges. Where do those beliefs come from? Experience determines what you believe works and doesn't work. Thoughts you've been told or taught that worked or didn't work for you, what makes you feel good and what hurts you—these are the foundations of the beliefs that inspire these rules.

To further illustrate how rules come from beliefs, consider the shark bait experiment. The story goes that a marine biologist put live bait in a tank with a shark, and as expected, the shark aggressively attacked the bait and ate it. After repeating this process a few times over the course of several days, the biologist changed things up on the hungry shark. She put a strong, clear barrier in the tank and then put the live bait on the other side of the barrier from the shark. The shark swam aggressively toward the bait and crashed into the clear barrier. The shark proceeded to repeat this behavior for an extended period of time until finally it stopped hitting the barrier and swam placidly around its side of the tank. In the final stage of the experiment, the biologist removed the clear barrier, yet the shark no longer attempted to get to the bait. Because of its experience crashing into the barrier and failing to get the food, the shark believed getting to the food was impossible. It continued to swim in the small pattern that had been available to it when the barrier was there, even after the barrier was gone. The shark had experienced its lack of access to the bait after a number of unsuccessful attempts, and from that, it formed the belief that it could not get to the bait, which led to the rule that it would not repeat the action of swimming in that part of the tank.

CHALLENGING PAST EXPERIENCES

The shark's behavior in this experiment is very similar to how people form rules based on beliefs founded upon past experiences and future expectations. What if, when you were younger, you tried out for a lead part in a school play, but instead were placed in the chorus? Then when you tried out again for the next show, and you still wound up in the chorus? Based on these experiences, what might you believe? You could form beliefs like the following:

- I'm just not lead part material.
- I can be trusted for smaller things, but experts believe I'm not up to handling major responsibilities.
- Drama is not for me.
- Putting yourself out there just leads to disappointment. Playing small is safer.

These are just examples, and there are many things you might come to believe. But for this discussion, say you form the aforementioned beliefs and that these subtly become your rules. Because you believe you're not lead part material, your rules might become:

- I won't put myself out there for the big parts
  (or apply to the big schools or seek a big promotion).
- I'll only work behind the scenes.
- I must do my best to be invisible.
- I will not attempt anything that makes me vulnerable to disappointment.
- I will only allow myself to make safe choices.

One of my daughters has ADHD and, when she was younger, struggled with trying to thrive in a traditional classroom. She was also introverted, and speaking out in an already uncomfortable environment stretched her, sometimes beyond capacity. Many children with ADHD struggle with multistep instructions. They might be on step one when others in the class are completing step seven, not because they are slow but because they are caught up in the details of step one; to make it even more challenging, if they are not interested in the assignment, they might be facing an internal battle as they work to devote extra energy to overcoming their natural resistance. One of the strategies she was taught was, whenever she felt lost, to look around at her classmates to see what they were doing in order to find clues that could inform her about what she should be doing. This was not a bad strategy in the context of a classroom, but in the larger world, it can be hard to discern when you should employ this strategy and when you should not. That was my daughter's experience.

So what belief might develop from an experience like this? Perhaps, "I'm wrong if I'm not doing what everyone else is doing." And what rule might come out of that? "I must measure myself by other people's behaviors and standards instead of trusting my own inner compass." For a long time, my daughter's choices were based on trying to match others' standards and behaviors with her own. Then there was the dilemma she faced of who she should be matching her behaviors and actions to. I know it wasn't easy for her to develop in confidence or to know how to trust herself. I'm grateful to share that she did find ways to trust herself; she learned, leaned into her own creativity, runs her own business today, and is a wonderful mother to my grandchildren. She is thriving these days, but she would tell you that we had some rough years of learning together.

Now, let's look at a different example. I have a client who, because of her childhood experiences of limited financial means, developed the belief that success was best judged by the money she brought in. You'll notice that this belief is not wrong, but it is also not complete. For my client, when her position was downsized, she strove hard to not only recoup her income but also prove her success by acquiring multiple businesses. She also became overwhelmed and burnt out. Her beliefs drove her to develop rules that dictated her behavior to the point that they became detrimental to her well-being. Through our work together, she realized that yes, money can be a measure of success, but it doesn't outweigh other measures—or at least, letting it outweigh those measures had put her in harm's way. Together, we mined for the beliefs that no longer aligned with her values, examined the possibility of other measures of success, and adjusted her beliefs. This empowered her to break her own rules and find other beliefs to drive her actions.

I don't want to give the impression that rules are bad. They are actually super helpful when they are based on current context. For example, take the rule that I will not watch a screen within thirty minutes of going to bed. This is based on the context of current research that says the light from televisions, phones, tablets, and other screens can make it difficult for our brains to shut down and sleep. The rule is generated by the belief that sleep is important, and I can take action to prioritize quality sleep. So in this case, the rule is highly beneficial.

As you may be beginning to see, rules go wrong when they are:

- Based on faulty intelligence that informed a belief. The intelligence either was never true or is no longer true.

- Applied with abandon instead of focused accurately. Some beliefs are contextual—remember my daughter, cuing off others in a classroom? It worked in a classroom context, but taking cues from others in life can be debilitating.

- Treated as absolutes, backed up by black-and-white thinking about a belief. It's the idea that a particular belief is 100 percent right, and any other belief is 100 percent wrong. When your beliefs are black-and-white, you create black-and-white rules that result in inflexibility and an inability to adapt to new circumstances or different goals.

Let's take an example from American history to illustrate the need for accurate and updated information. In 1961, President John F. Kennedy and the CIA supported an invasion of Cuba to oust Fidel Castro, carried out by 1,400 Cuban exiles. It failed, and this was a stinging and embarrassing defeat for the Kennedy administration, so he looked for ways to avoid repeating this type of failure. One factor that he believed contributed to the failure was the lack of current information. From this, he established the White House Situation Room so that the president could have access to intelligence as it is gathered. He recognized the error of relying on out-of-date information. Things change. What is true one moment may not be true the next. Similarly, you need to give yourself permission to gather your own up-to-date information and verify the truths upon which you are basing your beliefs before you create rules around them. And like President Kennedy, you need to make sure you are checking in regularly so that your information is accurate and current. You need a "beliefs situation room."

BELIEFS PRE-FLIGHT CHECK

As I mentioned earlier, beliefs take time to develop, and aligning your beliefs and goals for effective flight also takes time. So that you're not overwhelmed in the process, let's do a Beliefs Pre-Flight Check to find out what beliefs may be holding you back. If you were a pilot working through a pre-flight checklist, you would look closely at the plane's systems and test each part to make sure it will support flight. What a pilot doesn't do is criticize the plane if something doesn't check out. Put aside self-judgment, use your endearment, and exercise compassion for yourself like you would for someone else you love dearly. To perform this pre-flight check, you need to understand your system of beliefs, the rules those beliefs support, the actions you take based on those rules, and the results those actions create. Check the following definitions to make sure you know what you're looking for.

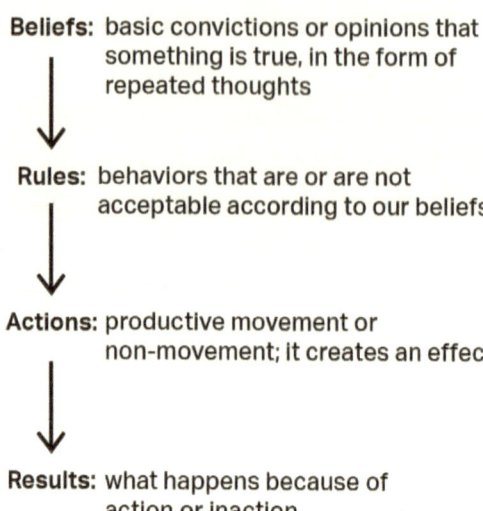

Image 15.1: Beliefs, Rules, Actions, and Results

By the previous definitions, you can see that based on your beliefs, you create rules that determine what actions you will or will not take, which in turn creates our results.

Now, have a look at the following inverse model. When we flip the model, you'll notice the foundation is the belief, but often what we notice first is the result. It's kind of like looking at an iceberg; you see what protrudes above the waterline, but what you see is created by what is actually unseen below the water. You may see some similarities with the FETBO Template; however, this work isn't looking at thought, feelings, or pointing to a specific circumstance. This work helps you home in on the beliefs and rules that may conflict with your goal and its supporting actions.

Image 15.2: Results, Actions, Rules, and Beliefs

Now that you have begun working on your goals, please choose a result you have noticed is slowing you down in your success, that you feel you are resisting, or that you are getting but do not want. You are looking to uncover the beliefs that hold you back from getting the results you want. Like working with the FETBO Template, sometimes results are easier to access than the beliefs that underpin them—they are more visible. So let's start with the results. Have a look at my following model where I've used the example of finishing this book. First, I fill out the model with the result I'm getting: This writing process is dragging on for months longer than I thought it would. Next, I record the action I'm taking that is creating the result.

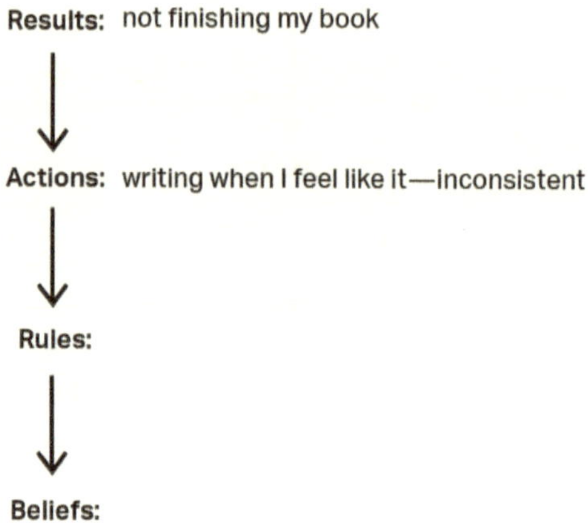

Results: not finishing my book

↓

Actions: writing when I feel like it—inconsistent

↓

Rules:

↓

Beliefs:

Image 15.3: Writing a Book Example

The first two lines are pretty easy but as I work my way down the model, I come to the rule that supports the action. This gets a bit more challenging because it is often easier to uncover the belief before you notice the rule. Don't let this challenge stop you; skip to the belief line because I have a simple (though not always easy) way to track down that troublesome belief. Pause your work on the Belief Model for just a minute and create a simple two-column work page.

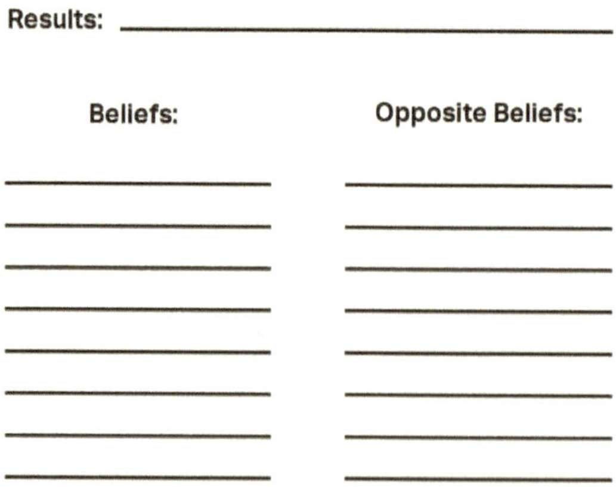

Results: _____

Beliefs:	**Opposite Beliefs:**
_____	_____
_____	_____
_____	_____
_____	_____
_____	_____
_____	_____
_____	_____

Image 15.4: Beliefs and Opposite Beliefs Work Page

Grab the result you put in your Belief Model and write that as a title at the top of your page. In the left column, generate a list of beliefs you have that could be creating the result you have filled in. Ask yourself, what belief(s) do I have that are creating this result? The key here is to ask yourself. You may even add your endearment: "Love, what is keeping you from finishing this book?" Notice you are looking for beliefs, not actions. Make a list just off the top of your head. It may be toward the bottom that the big reasons really start showing up. For example:

- There isn't enough time.
- Family crisis needs my attention.
- No one will actually read it, so why bother?
- There are already a million books out there.
- I start things, but I'm not a good finisher.
- I need to pay the bills, and there is little money in publishing a book.

As you look toward the end of the list, you'll notice the deeper reasons. Now, in the column on the right side of your page, make a list of the opposite of those beliefs.

- There is as much time as I choose to give it.
- I can support my family and still have time and energy to write.
- The message of this book will be of interest and helpful to many people.
- There are millions of readers out there.
- I am a great finisher.
- My finances can improve not only with the publication of my book but with new clients who find me and my work through reading my book.

That's a lot of new beliefs to try to take on, so your next step is to choose the one that can create the biggest change to your results. How do you determine this? Work down your list of reasons and try them on with an "if . . . then I will" statement. This is the one that stuck for me: "If I believe that I am a great finisher, then I will create and honor a writing schedule with fierce resolve." That one felt like it would create the result I wanted of finishing my book by my birthday. Okay, now go back to your Beliefs Model. Fill out the old belief and then the rule you created based on that belief. Remember, rules are behaviors that are or are not acceptable according to our beliefs. Actions are productive movements and non-movements that create an effect, are based on the internal guidebook of our beliefs, and define what is "allowed" or "forbidden" according to our rules.

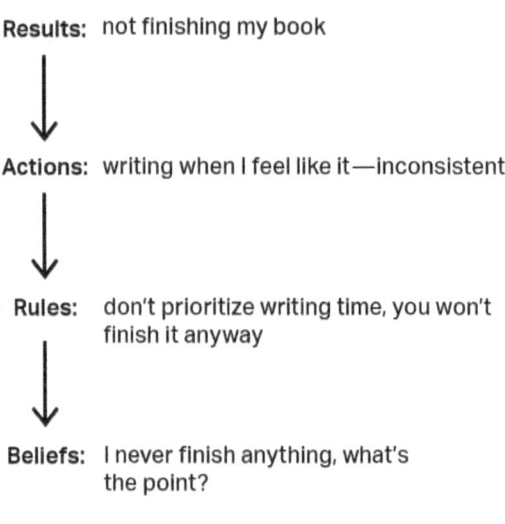

Image 15.5: Writing a Book Example

In my example, you can see how the system of my belief and my rule created the undesirable result that opposed my goal. Now that I've sleuthed that out, I get to create a new version of the Belief Model with my updated belief. You'll notice that completing the "if . . . then

I will" statement can fill out the action line of my new Beliefs Model, and the same could also be used in my FETBO Template in the action line to help add the power of feelings and continue to unpack my next steps. Keep working your "if . . . then" exercise until you also have your action line populated. All that is left is the rule. To fill in your rule, think about what it would be like to live by that belief. What rule could apply to every situation if you live by that belief? For me, it was "I can take on any project I choose without fear of letting myself or someone else down because I know I will finish it."

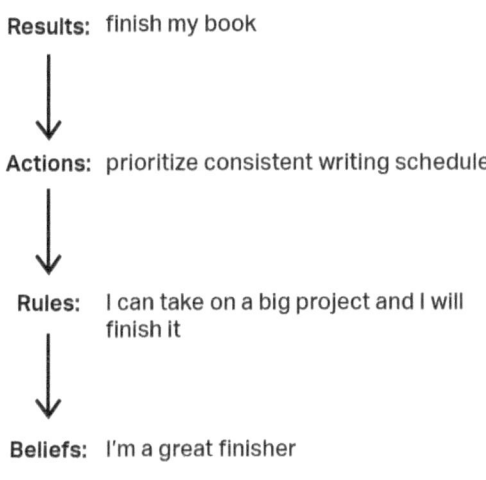

Image 15.6: Writing a Book Example

This is the completed process, but even though it sounds simple, and it kind of is, remember that your beliefs come from your experiences and expectations. Sometimes, replacing a belief can be a lot harder in practice than it is in principle. Take a look at the evidence supporting the old belief, so you can instead provide evidence of the new belief. Is the old evidence true? Even if it is true, is there another belief that is equally true that would serve you better by moving you toward the result you want? Some practitioners would say this is unnecessary—looking back is unfruitful and can be painful. I'd argue that learning from your past can be very fruitful, and while looking at past events can be painful, you know from your permission to feel work that painful emotions deliver valuable messages that you can leverage to move forward. While camping in your past victories (living on past successes and longing for things to be just like they were before) is not a helpful practice, as a nonjudgmental observer, you can discover the evidence supporting the old belief that may or may not have served an important purpose at one time, but no longer supports you now. This is the work you are going to do. But be encouraged; you're not in it alone.

Let's approach that old belief to determine its veracity. Using my example, what evidence supports my belief that I'm not a great finisher? Well, at first, when I ask myself that question, I look at the unfinished projects around my home. Then I think about my list of things I wanted to do but didn't take on because I was afraid I wouldn't finish them. Then I think about the times I've disappointed people because I didn't finish something. That is enough, and while it may be uncomfortable, looking at this evidence is really helpful for collecting new evidence. Because this is not therapy, you are not looking at wounds that show up in this process. However, if you do find sensitive areas or uncover some wounds through this work, that is an indication to find a qualified therapist who can help you pursue healing.

FINDING EVIDENCE OF YOUR BELIEFS

Remember: Your job is not to judge or blame. Remind yourself that you see memories through your own lens. Stay away from blame while being curious about where your brain is finding evidence to maintain a belief. Beliefs are in your control bucket, and you do not have to let anyone else's beliefs take up residence there. So here's the thing about your amazing brain: When you form a belief, your brain begins to endlessly search for evidence that backs up that belief. Remember the RAS? A belief is a thought you have repeated enough that your brain has been trained to focus only on evidence that supports that belief. You have given that thought so much attention that your RAS has filtered out most of what would contradict that belief.

Think of this as entering a topic into a search engine. If you enter "chocolate cake recipe" into Google, you will instantly see images and recipes both new and old from all over the internet. When I began my quest to search out the evidence for my old belief that I'm not a great finisher, my brain easily provided the supporting facts because it has been accumulating evidence since the belief's inception. This was a deeply ingrained belief with a lot of evidence behind it. But if I decide it's time to let go of that belief, I have several tools at my disposal.

The first tool is the list we generated earlier in this chapter. You have identified not only an old belief but in your opposites list, you have formulated a new belief that is more aligned with your goals and values. Make sure that, similar to your thought in the FETBO Template, your new belief is believable. For example, if my new belief is that I could play in the WNBA, and my rule is to play in every tryout the WNBA hosts, I will not be able to collect evidence to support that belief. I'm a 5'3", fifty-six-year-old woman who has never played in a competitive basketball game. Align your beliefs with your prioritized goals and your values, and make sure they are believable. Your believable belief may be somewhere in between your current belief and the opposite belief you identified. Do the work and determine your new belief.

As I mentioned earlier, to help replace my old belief with all its evidence, I must focus on finding new evidence to support my new belief. Yes, when I finish my book, it will add to the evidence, but I want to start to immediately create that new evidence file. First, I look for things I've finished. Yep, there are plenty. I've finished my high school and college degrees. I have finished making thousands of great (at least most of them) meals, and my kids have never gone hungry. I have finished many home projects. I have finished my coaching certification requirements. I have finished a fiction book. I have finished a number of plays and short articles. I have finished a series of kids' books. The list is actually quite long, and I think you've got the point.

The next tool is changing the label. In my old beliefs, I was identifying as a quitter. This is an example of the identity that goes with a belief. I want to refer to myself as a finisher. And, by the way, you are looking for *being* identity anchors. The evidence may consist of things you've done, but when you go to adopt a new identity label, you may as well do the work of adopting a label that is not only based on what you are currently doing but also who you are showing up as; that way it can translate into different contexts. I want to take a moment to remind you that these are identity anchors that you are intentionally engaging. But the thing about anchors is that the captain of the boat (the person who has permission) decides where to drop them and when to pull them in. You are that captain. With our work here identifying supportive beliefs, you are also working to clarify supportive identity anchors. When an anchor no longer allows the desired forward movement, it's time to pull it in.

Back to the work of supporting your new belief with a being identifier. Instead of using your endearment in your self-talk, you want to call yourself by that identifier—in my case, a finisher. In this way, you are tuning in the RAS to help see the evidence your new belief needs. Feeling discouraged about taking on your next big task? Imagine saying to yourself, "You'll never get this done. You'll make a big mess and then walk away like you always do." Notice the thoughts you might have as a result and catch them based on your chosen belief. What if you were to replace that inner statement with, "Think it through. Remember all the things you've finished, all the people you've supported by finishing. Listen, finisher, you can do this. You're a strong finisher." Another tool you can use to build up your evidence is to set small doable deadlines, quick wins that you call out in your self-talk. "Look, there you go—finishing again."

Back to the book example: My coach and I set up the idea of having writing "two-a-days," meaning two different writing times a day. When I got my two touches on my book a day, I had finished my two-a-day goal. You caught that, right? I finished my goal . . . because I'm a finisher.

THE POWER OF LIMITING BELIEFS

As you travel back to check the context and veracity of your beliefs, watch out for "I am" statements. For example, "I am an unstructured person, so I can only behave in an unstructured way." Statements like this are huge limiting beliefs and correspond to identity anchors that often will not serve you. When you allow an inaccurate and finite label to define your belief, you are exercising a fixed mindset and slipping into a variation of the blame habit discussed earlier. Remember: If you don't own it, you can't alter it. If you attribute a label as fixed in place, like a structural wall that can't be torn down, then you are limiting yourself.

According to Stanford University professor Carol Dweck, a fixed mindset is when "people believe their basic qualities, like their intelligence or talent, are simply fixed traits. They spend their time documenting their intelligence or talent instead of developing them. They also believe that talent alone creates success—without effort."[1] The opposite of a fixed mindset is a growth mindset. This is when people believe that their most basic abilities can be developed through dedication and hard work—brains and talent are just the starting point.

I remember when we renovated our master bathroom. We live in a 1970s Dutch Colonial–style house that had not been updated since it was built. Our master bathroom was separated from the bedroom by a half wall where the sink and cabinet resided and a pocket door opening onto a 3x6 foot (carpeted) room that contained the toilet and a 3x3 foot shower. We had wanted to renovate it for about ten years and were finally moved to action because the shower was leaking into the entryway below. What does this have to do with a fixed mindset? Well, we had several designers give us ideas and then bid on the project. I knew I wanted to make the half wall into a full-height wall and add a door, so the vanity lights did not shine into the bedroom while one of us was getting ready in the morning and the other one was trying to sleep. I also knew

I wanted to stop the flow of water through the ceiling and get rid of the bathroom carpet (gross!). I had resigned myself to the 3x3 shower and toilet closet combo. All but one of the designers presented plans that met those desires with nice finishes and new lighting. The last designer looked at our space and then asked if she could open our fairly small walk-in closet that had a window and shared a wall with our current bathroom. She looked at me and said, "We can do what you've asked, but if you want, I can also bid to switch the closet and the bathroom space. We can utilize the same plumbing and get you a bigger bathroom, maybe even a tub." What?! I hadn't seen that possibility at all because in my mind, the space we already had as the bathroom was set. I had never considered more than an update. When she presented this relatively simple solution, the options opened wide.

When you notice an "I am" statement as you do this work, check the label. It might be a belief that is still supporting your growth, but like our old, carpeted bathroom, it might be a belief that is holding you back and is totally changeable.

Let's check in with where you are in our journey to flight. We've learned how to identify the beliefs that tether us, and we've learned how to untether ourselves. How's the air up there? Even if you are not soaring yet, hopefully, your feet have left the ground in some area of chosen impact. We've also started construction on the "beliefs situation room," and now it's time to put it to use. I want to offer one more flight support for your journey.

BELIEFS COLLECTIVE

When working through the Beliefs Model, you took a specific result that you wanted but were not getting. That is continuing work, my friend. It's a very results-oriented approach that brings about quick change. In this chapter, you are still looking at beliefs, but now are examining them systematically and storing them accessibly. Similar

Practicing the Principles of Flying

to how you created a Library of Emotions, you want to create a Beliefs Collective or our very own situation room. You already have many beliefs in your collective, but now that you know how to identify and alter your beliefs, it's time to get intentional about cleaning out and updating your collection. Like your old parachute pants (which are back in style—who'd have thought?) or your high school letter jacket, beliefs get out of date, no longer fit, or just don't work for our current lives.

You can use the model from the last chapter if you need help uncovering your beliefs based on the results you're getting in each area, especially if you want to change the results you're getting. Sometimes, you're happy with the results in an area, and you can uncover those beliefs by simply asking yourself what they are. You'll want to hang on to those. Additionally, when working with beliefs, it is important to remember that some beliefs will never change, as they will always support the results you want. The whole point of building the collective is to pull together your many current and updated beliefs in one place. So, utilize the downloadable Beliefs Collective page through the QR code on the table of tools at the front of the book, or open a fresh new journal or notebook and get started.

Remember: Don't judge your beliefs. You are observing and collecting. Similar to the Marie Kondo method of cleaning out your closet, you start by piling everything on your bed before you decide what to keep and what to let go of based on how much joy it gives you. Don't limit yourself to only asking how beliefs make you feel; also ask if they are supporting the actions you need to create impactful flight. I will tell you, however, that the Marie Kondo method bothers me a little because of the mess it makes. If you follow her approach to the letter, you can't sleep in your bed until you get it done. The point at which you have all your things on your bed just makes you feel like you want to quit, move houses, or at least go sleep somewhere else. These are feelings. Feelings are human. Be compassionate and curious with whatever feelings come up, and you will not be afraid of them. You know how to process uncomfortable feelings. All this to say, you can do this work over time. You don't have to pile all these thoughts on your bed and not take a break until it's done. Remember also that you have the model from the last chapter to use for specific hot spots. You can get immediate belief shift with it.

With this work, you are playing the long game. This work will help you function with more clarity, motivation, and, yes, joy in each area of your life. Start with the following list to mine for beliefs in each area. Feel free to record any rules that show up (rules are actions you take or won't take based on a belief). This is to just to expand awareness and continue to build muscle. Remember: You don't have to do this all in one go. It can be the work of a few minutes, hours, weeks, or months.

These following categories offer a starting point to help you explore, update, and organize your Beliefs Collective. Go at your own pace. This is an expansive exercise, and since you want to stay up to date, it's not all part of a permanent collection. Think about closet cleaning—your closets rarely stay as organized as they were at first, and clothes often go out of style or size.

> **Be compassionate and curious with whatever feelings come up, and you will not be afraid of them.**

IDENTITY BELIEFS

- **Body**: How you feel about your appearance, energy, ability to heal, flexibility
- **Mind**: How sharp you feel mentally; your ability to learn
- **Spirit**: How you fit in the universe; your relationship with God or higher power

- **Emotions:** How you deal with your emotions; how you express your feelings

RELATIONSHIP BELIEFS

- **Family:** How you interact with your family
- **Friends:** What kind of friend you are; what kind of friends you have
- **Romance:** Your worthiness for romance; how you create romance

MONEY BELIEFS

- **Earning:** How much you can earn and in what ways
- **Saving/Investing:** What you do to grow what you earn
- **Giving:** What amount to give, to whom, and how you decide

SERVICE BELIEFS

- **Who:** The group or cause where you want to create impact
- **What:** Ways you can help that group or cause
- **Value:** How you create value for others in your home, community, planet
- **Gifts:** Strengths that support your service
- **Weaknesses:** Traits that stand in the way of your service

FUTURE BELIEFS

- **Hope:** What positive ideas do you have about the future
- **Plans:** What you intend to do moving forward

- **Legacy:** What you believe about the value you will leave behind

Feel free to add other categories, but these cover some foundational beliefs for our purposes. Now it's time to see if those beliefs are serving you. Go back to the first belief you wrote down and check the rules and results it is creating. If you haven't plugged it into the Belief Model, now is the time to do so. Most of our beliefs come from early experiences, and sometimes they are even the beliefs of others that you have adopted without question. Now is the time to question them. Do they still fit? Did they ever fit? Is your belief creating the results you want?

BELIEF CHECKLIST

- Have you used it lately?
- Is it creating the results you want?
- Is it a solid foundation for rules that move you toward your flight goals?
- Is it something you would want your child or protégé to believe?
- Does it give you energy?
- What emotions does it inspire in you?
- What actions does it motivate you to take? Do those actions align with your values?

As with the other skills you have learned in this book, keeping your beliefs updated takes flexing those muscles. The work gets easier the more you practice, but it is work. Remember to tap into your flight plan (goals you set before you started this work) and imagine what your future self will feel and accomplish when you have a clean and clear Beliefs Collective. Do this work consistently to create a compound effect of moving into flight. Remember that you have permission to put in the time and energy to do this work.

One example of a motivating belief is a quote from Billy Jean King that is posted at the entrance of the players' tunnel leading to the court at the US Open in Flushing Meadows, New York. The quote reads, "Pressure is a privilege," and it is the last thing players see before they walk onto the tennis court. Often, you'll see a player touch the message to physically connect with this belief as they go by. I would love to interview them and ask what actions that belief inspired. I imagine you would hear some powerful stories. If you believed that "pressure is a privilege," what rules would you create?

GROWTH ISN'T COMFORTABLE

Let's dig deeper into the concept of Beliefs Collectives using the topic of money. In the earnings category of the money beliefs mentioned earlier, the question came up: How much can you earn and in what way? Before my coaching practice, I never earned more than $30,000 per year. This feels super shocking as I see it in writing, but to give a little context, before setting up my own company, the last time I drew a paycheck was in the early 1990s. Starting in 1994, I was a stay-at-home mom producing no income for twenty years. I did, however, spend a lot of time and energy volunteering in schools and churches. So, my coaches and I had a lot of work to do to get me to value my time enough to make a living in my current line of work. When I took on the task of examining my beliefs, right at the start of my own business, here are a few that showed up:

- I'm just a stay-at-home mom. What value can I give to my clients?
- Sure, I have a degree, but psychology is more of a service industry and you don't make much.
- I love helping people, and a good person does that for free.

- I'm not a good saver, so I don't deserve to be wealthy.
- No one in my family has ever been wealthy. It's easy if you start with family money.
- Having money would change me and the way people think of me.
- I only feel justified spending money on someone else.
- Smart people put money in their savings account to be ready for a rainy day.

I freely admit that when I revisit my old beliefs about money, I can see how they no longer serve me. But don't get tripped up on whether my former beliefs were right or trying to figure out why I formed them in the first place. Notice what you feel when you read my old beliefs. Did you shake your head or say, "What's wrong with that?" Take care not to slip into judgmentalism; it smothers creativity and growth—both yours and others'. And if you're like me, you sometimes judge yourself more harshly than anyone else. Also like me, you may sometimes judge everyone but yourself. Aren't humans an interesting mix of contrasts? No matter how you judge, remember: You will never reach your potential for creativity and growth when you allow judgmentalism to flourish in your mind. Be aware that being judgmental can creep in when you're distracted or tired or stressed, such as when you aren't getting the results you want and feel like flying is not something you can achieve. If this is a struggle for you, revisit the challenges to flight section about judgment and judgmentalism.

Here's is an example of the Beliefs Model with the results from my old money beliefs:

Image 15.7: Coaching Example

I'm not always comfortable sharing from my own experience as an example, but you and I both know that growth isn't comfortable. I did the work at the time, but even years later, I still work to provide evidence for my new belief. Here is how my new belief translated into a rule, which supported action that created very different results.

> You will never reach your potential for creativity and growth when you allow judgmentalism to flourish in your mind.

Image 15.8: Coaching Example

I want to make sure you hear this loud and clear: To achieve goals and create powerful impact, you need to **approach** your beliefs and the rules they inspire, **adjust** based on more accurate information and goals, and **act** in a way that aligns with your values and creates the desired impact.

MEASURE YOUR PROGRESS

Let's take a minute and check in on your permission to fly. Notice, once again, to stay out of self-judgment. This is a measurement of progress, and we celebrate progress, not perfection. No matter how you answer here, you are taking actions toward flight. Read the following statements and rate yourself on a scale of 1–10, with 1 being "I don't agree" and 10 being "I strongly agree with this statement."

- I can trust myself to recognize and prevent imposter syndrome.
- I can notice beliefs that no longer support my values and vision for how I choose to show up.
- I can adjust my beliefs to support my success.
- I can imagine and express what I want to create impact for myself and others.
- My identity is clear and anchored in my values and goals.
- I have a golden circle of support and accountability.
- I can fly.

Notice any place where you don't strongly agree with these statements. What work do you need to do to firm up your agreement?

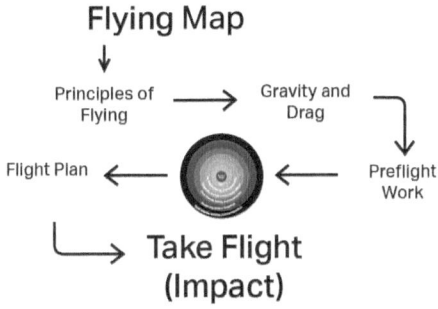

Image 11.1: Permission to Fly Map

ALL SYSTEMS GO

You now have the systems to support flight. Put it all together, my journeying friend. Hold tight to the principles of approach, adjust, and act as you create your flight plan by fixing your eyes on your destination. Put your destination in your pre-sight model. Write down your steps, listing out the actions that support success. Make those actions into goals, make them SMART (specific, measurable, actionable, relevant, and timebound), and schedule them on your calendar. Lean into your golden circle for support and accountability. Have courage and trust yourself to value and process the emotions that show up, focus on and feed the feelings and thoughts that support your desired outcomes, and adjust beliefs to be supportive as you move upward. You can do this because you have given yourself permission.

TAKEAWAYS

- **A belief is a basic conviction or opinion that something is true in the form of repeated thought, and a rule is behavior that is or is not acceptable according to your beliefs.** Based on their beliefs, humans create rules about how they will or will not act. People form rules based on their past experiences and future expectations.

- This can become **a problem when your rules are based on faulty intelligence that either was never true or is no longer true, are applied with abandon instead of focused accurately, or are treated as absolutes** because of the black-and-white thinking behind a belief. If you hold a limiting belief, you will create rules to limit yourself and reinforce that belief.

- To avoid those outcomes, **work through the Beliefs Model as a pre-flight check.** Home in on any beliefs and rules that may conflict with your goal and its supporting actions. You are looking to build awareness of the beliefs that hold you back from getting the results you want.

- **Replace a limiting belief with one capable of making the biggest impact on your end goal.** To fill in your rule, think about what it would be like to live by that impactful belief. What rule could apply to every situation if you live by that belief?

- **Change your old limiting beliefs by changing the label you use for yourself** and the evidence you look for to support that identity. Anchor your identity in how you are showing up, not just what you do.
- When you allow an inaccurate and finite label to define your belief, you are exercising a **fixed mindset**. Remember: If you don't own it, you can't alter it. If you attribute a label as fixed in place, like a structural wall that can't be torn down, then you are limiting yourself. **The opposite of a fixed mindset is a growth mindset.** This is when people believe that their abilities can be developed through dedication and hard work.
- Just as you built a Library of Emotions, it's time to create a **Beliefs Collective**. You already hold many beliefs, but now that you can identify and reshape them, be intentional about refining and updating them. Organize your beliefs in categories—identity, relationships, money, service, and the future—while questioning whether they truly serve you.
- **Growth isn't comfortable**, but take care not to slip into judgmentalism as you examine your beliefs; it smothers creativity and growth—both yours and others'. You will never reach your potential for creativity and growth when you allow judgmentalism to flourish in your mind.
- To **achieve goals and create powerful impact**, you need to **approach** your beliefs and the rules they inspire, **adjust** based on more accurate information and goals, and **act** in a way that aligns with your values and creates the impact you desire.

NEXT STEPS:

The Continuing Practice of Permission

You have come to the end of our journey in these pages, yet you are actually just beginning the next phase. Before you close this book, take a moment with the following graphic. Appreciate the ground you have covered and how it all comes together to produce feelings fitness, resilient authenticity, and impactful results. Keep up your work with the skills you've developed and the tools you've mastered. Even if some of the tools here may not have been the best fit for your current season, I encourage you to revisit each permission regularly. Change is constant, and some tools you don't need for this particular hike may be exactly the right ones to pick up on the next leg of your journey. Practice the principles of permission to produce the results you want. (I did mention I like alliteration.)

Permission

	Feel	Fail	Fly
Approach	Build emotional literacy	Failure/success analysis	Flight dreams
Adjust	To more supportive emotions	To leverage learning	To clear goals and accurate beliefs
Act	Choose action with pyramid work	Take adjusted action to try again	Take flight with pre-flight strategy
	Fitness	Authenticity	Impact

Principles (vertical axis) / **Product** (horizontal axis)

Image 16.1: Principles of Permission

As I said in the very beginning, you are chosen, authorized, and purposed with showing up in your life with authenticity and impact. I want to add just one more adjective to that line: equipped. Because of the work you have done, you are chosen, authorized, purposed, and equipped to show up in your life with authenticity and impact.

My final request of you is to make sure you are sharing your journey. The permissions you give yourself can inspire others to embrace their own permission. This is how it works to make this planet a better place to live now and in the future. You don't have to tackle the whole world on your own to make a difference. Create a ripple effect by impacting your part of it. And it all starts with giving yourself these three permissions.

My friend, we are just about done with our journey together, but something has been at play through the pages that I want to help you recognize. Each permission has started with a Mission Mindset. I explained at the beginning that I was pointing those out from the start so that you know the mindset needed for that particular permission. I didn't choose the title Mission Mindset lightly. I now want you to notice that hidden within permission is the word **mission**, reminding us that granting ourselves permission is an active choice, a deliberate journey toward something important. When we give ourselves permission, we're not only allowing ourselves to act or feel; we're actually stepping onto a path with purpose, intention, and direction. By embracing the Mission Mindset, you consciously committed to the meaningful exploration of your potential. Notice each mindset isn't passive—it's a courageous declaration that you are both the creator and explorer of your own experience. Permission, then, becomes not just an act of allowing, but a powerful launching point for your **per**sonal mission.

It is a poignant moment for me as I pen these final words to you, dear fellow traveler. I wish I could walk by your side as you hike your own Grand Canyon—planning your route, navigating challenges, checking off milestones, and taking in the view. Just remember, the most important aspect of this journey isn't getting to the destination but who you become along the way. However, I know that you can do it, you will make it, and in my heart, I am waiting at the other rim to witness your ascent. I am applauding loudly as you take flight and change the world for the better. You'll know it's me cheering you on. I'll be the one with the squeaky shoes.

RECOMMENDED RESOURCES

Emotional Agility: Get Unstuck, Embrace Change, and Thrive in Work and Life by Susan David

Mindset: The New Psychology of Success by Carol S. Dweck

Change Your Questions, Change Your Life, 4th Edition: 12 Powerful Tools for Leadership, Coaching, and Results by Marilee Adams, PhD

How to Be an Imperfectionist: The New Way to Self-Acceptance, Fearless Living, and Freedom from Perfectionism by Stephen Guise

Own Your Greatness: Overcome Impostor Syndrome, Beat Self-Doubt, and Succeed in Life by Dr. Lisa Orbé-Austin, PhD and Dr. Richard Orbé-Austin, PhD

Acknowledgments

I'm so grateful for my husband, Mike, and my daughters, Andrea, Michaela, and Kennedy, as well as my parents, Dan and Sheryl Smith. Each of you encouraged, celebrated, and nurtured me through this process.

Thank you to my friends (Sabine and Jill) and clients who shared your journeys to lead yourselves and help others along the way. And to my talented friend Sophie Beierle for your beautiful work on the author photo.

Thanks also to the whole Greenleaf publishing team: Jessica Choi for adding structure with your wisdom and gentle feedback. Amanda Elysse Hughes for keeping me focused and supporting the reader journey. Kimberly Lance for leveraging your artistic talent for the beautiful cover and interior design. Morgan Robinson for pulling all the pieces into a cohesive unit. Tenyia Lee for catching stumbling blocks and turning them into stepping stones. Leah Pierre for keeping everything on track and getting us across the finish line. You all excelled in your roles and were generous sounding boards. Your support helped me feel like not only a coach with a message but also a writer.

Every person mentioned and many I'm sure I left out (please forgive me) played a pivotal role in the inception and creation of this work, and I don't just mean this book—I mean the work of me. I am humbled by your belief and support. Thank you so much for helping me give myself permission.

APPENDIX 1:
Emotions Thesaurus

You can use this Emotions Thesaurus to help you build your emotional literacy. This collection is based on the Three Permissions Feelings Wheel, and, while not exhaustive, it can be a good starting point for you to label and identify your feelings. Each entry includes a definition, an example of possible physical sensations, and common body language expressions. Tip: As you work your way through, use the body language expressions to "try on" the emotion by mirroring with your own posture.

1. ACCEPTED
Definition: Feeling acknowledged, valued, and included by others.
Physical Sensations: Warmth in the chest, relaxed muscles, steady heartbeat.
Body Language: Open posture, slight smile, making eye contact, leaning slightly toward others.

2. ACCEPTING
Definition: Being open to situations, people, or feelings without resistance.
Physical Sensations: Lightness in the chest, ease in breathing, relaxed shoulders.
Body Language: Nodding, open palms, gentle eye contact, soft facial expressions.

3. AGGRESSIVE
Definition: Acting in a forceful or confrontational manner, often with hostility.
Physical Sensations: Increased heart rate, tense jaw, adrenaline surge.
Body Language: Clenched fists, narrowed eyes, forward-leaning posture, flared nostrils.

4. ALARMED
Definition: A sudden awareness of danger or threat.
Physical Sensations: Racing heartbeat, cold sweat, tight chest, adrenaline spike.
Body Language: Wide eyes, open mouth, tense shoulders, recoiling or freezing.

5. AMAZED
Definition: Overwhelmed by wonder or admiration.
Physical Sensations: Tingling sensation, raised eyebrows, slight gasp, expanded chest.
Body Language: Eyes widening, mouth slightly open, hands reaching out, upright posture.

6. ANGER
Definition: A strong feeling of displeasure or hostility.
Physical Sensations: Increased body temperature, clenched jaw, fast breathing.
Body Language: Furrowed brows, tight lips, fists clenched, rigid posture.

7. ANGST
Definition: A deep feeling of anxiety or dread, often existential in nature.
Physical Sensations: Tight stomach, shallow breathing, restlessness.
Body Language: Slumped posture, avoiding eye contact, fidgeting, rubbing hands together.

8. ANNOYED
Definition: Mild irritation or discomfort.
Physical Sensations: Tightness in the face, tension in shoulders, quickened pulse.
Body Language: Rolling eyes, sighing, crossing arms, tapping fingers.

9. ANXIOUS
Definition: Experiencing unease or nervousness about an uncertain outcome.
Physical Sensations: Racing heart, cold hands, shallow breathing, stomach knots.
Body Language: Fidgeting, avoiding eye contact, biting nails, pacing.

10. APPRECIATED
Definition: Feeling valued and recognized for one's contributions.
Physical Sensations: Warm chest, relaxed breathing, gentle heartbeat.
Body Language: Smiling, direct eye contact, upright posture, open gestures.

11. ASHAMED
Definition: Feeling guilty or embarrassed about one's actions.
Physical Sensations: Warm or flushed face, sinking stomach, tight throat.
Body Language: Looking down, avoiding eye contact, slumped posture, fidgeting.

12. AWE
Definition: A mix of wonder and fear or reverence in response to something powerful.
Physical Sensations: Breathlessness, chills, lightheadedness.
Body Language: Wide eyes, still posture, open mouth, deep breathing.

13. BELIEF
Definition: A strong conviction or trust in something or someone.
Physical Sensations: Steady heart rate, grounded feeling, relaxed body.
Body Language: Upright posture, firm eye contact, nodding, steady voice.

14. BETRAYED
Definition: Feeling deceived or let down by someone trusted.
Physical Sensations: Tight chest, heavy limbs, nausea.
Body Language: Crossed arms, avoiding eye contact, clenched jaw, stiff movements.

15. BITTER
Definition: Deep resentment or anger over a perceived wrong.
Physical Sensations: Tense jaw, stomach tightness, increased heart rate.
Body Language: Crossed arms, pursed lips, narrowed eyes, turning away from others.

16. BLISS
Definition: A state of pure joy and contentment.
Physical Sensations: Lightness in the body, warmth in the chest, deep breathing.
Body Language: Relaxed posture, genuine smile, bright eyes, fluid movements.

17. BORED
Definition: Feeling unstimulated or uninterested.
Physical Sensations: Heavy eyelids, restlessness, lack of energy.
Body Language: Slouching, yawning, fidgeting, lack of eye contact.

18. CALM
Definition: A state of peacefulness and tranquility.
Physical Sensations: Slow heartbeat, steady breathing, relaxed muscles.
Body Language: Open posture, steady gaze, slow movements, soft facial expressions.

19. COMPASSION
Definition: Feeling empathy and concern for others.
Physical Sensations: Warm chest, relaxed breath, gentle heartbeat.
Body Language: Soft eyes, open arms, leaning in, offering comforting gestures.

20. COMPETENT
Definition: Feeling capable and skilled in a task or ability.
Physical Sensations: Energized body, upright posture, steady breathing.
Body Language: Confident stance, direct eye contact, controlled hand gestures.

21. CONFIDENCE
Definition: A sense of trust in one's own abilities or qualities.
Physical Sensations: Expanded chest, steady breathing, light energy.
Body Language: Head held high, direct eye contact, purposeful gestures, relaxed shoulders.

22. CONTENT
Definition: Feeling peaceful and satisfied with one's current state.
Physical Sensations: Warmth in the chest, light breathing, stillness.
Body Language: Gentle smile, relaxed posture, hands resting comfortably.

23. CONTRARY
Definition: Inclined to disagree or oppose.
Physical Sensations: Tension in jaw and shoulders, elevated heartbeat.
Body Language: Crossed arms, shaking head, raised eyebrows.

24. CREATIVE
Definition: Feeling inspired to generate new ideas or solutions.
Physical Sensations: Lightness, openness in chest, buzzing energy.
Body Language: Animated gestures, wide eyes, open posture.

25. CREDITABLE
Definition: Feeling deserving of acknowledgment or praise.
Physical Sensations: Steady heartbeat, warmth in chest, light breath.
Body Language: Straight posture, calm facial expression, gentle smile.

26. CURIOUS
Definition: Wanting to learn or understand more about something.
Physical Sensations: Heightened alertness, quickened pulse, light breath.
Body Language: Leaning forward, raised eyebrows, focused eyes.

27. DAUNTLESS
Definition: Feeling courageous and resolute in the face of difficulty.
Physical Sensations: Strong heartbeat, steady breathing, feeling centered.
Body Language: Upright stance, direct gaze, squared shoulders.

28. DEFENSELESS
Definition: Feeling exposed and unable to protect oneself.
Physical Sensations: Tight chest, weak limbs, shallow breath.
Body Language: Shrinking posture, hunched shoulders, downcast eyes.

29. DELIGHT
Definition: A feeling of great pleasure and happiness.
Physical Sensations: Lightness, tingling, increased energy.
Body Language: Bright eyes, genuine smile, open gestures.

30. DEPRESSED
Definition: A persistent feeling of sadness or emptiness.
Physical Sensations: Heaviness in chest, fatigue, shallow breathing.
Body Language: Slumped posture, little eye contact, slow movements.

31. DISAPPOINTED
Definition: Feeling let down or unfulfilled by an expectation.
Physical Sensations: Heavy chest, weak limbs, shallow breath.
Body Language: Slumped posture, downcast gaze, tight lips.

32. DISAPPOINTING
Definition: A situation or event that fails to meet expectations.
Physical Sensations: Tightness in throat, sinking feeling in stomach.
Body Language: Slouched posture, sighing, lack of engagement.

33. DISGRACE
Definition: Feeling shame or dishonor due to one's actions.
Physical Sensations: Tight throat, flushed face, sinking stomach.
Body Language: Avoiding eye contact, head bowed, fidgeting.

34. DISMISSIVE
Definition: Showing indifference or lack of interest.
Physical Sensations: Tension in face, mild discomfort, shallow breath.
Body Language: Eye-rolling, turning away, crossing arms.

35. DISORIENTED
Definition: Feeling confused or uncertain about one's surroundings.
Physical Sensations: Dizziness, lightheadedness, unsteady breath.
Body Language: Furrowed brows, looking around, unsteady movements.

36. DISRESPECTED
Definition: Feeling disregarded or treated with lack of dignity.
Physical Sensations: Tight jaw, elevated heart rate, tense stomach.
Body Language: Crossed arms, narrowed eyes, avoiding eye contact.

37. DISTANT
Definition: Feeling emotionally or physically disconnected from others.
Physical Sensations: Numbness, lack of energy, slow heartbeat.
Body Language: Arms crossed, looking away, minimal facial expression.

38. DREAD
Definition: An overwhelming fear or unease about a future event.
Physical Sensations: Tight chest, rapid heartbeat, cold sweat.
Body Language: Hunched posture, wide eyes, fidgeting.

39. EMBARRASSED
Definition: Feeling awkward or self-conscious due to one's actions.
Physical Sensations: Flushed face, increased heart rate, tense stomach.
Body Language: Covering face, looking down, fidgeting, forced smile.

40. ENERGIZED
Definition: Feeling full of vitality and motivation.
Physical Sensations: Buzzing energy, increased heart rate, lightness in limbs.
Body Language: Upright posture, animated gestures, bright eyes.

41. ENGAGED
Definition: Feeling mentally or emotionally involved in an activity or conversation.
Physical Sensations: Steady heartbeat, sense of focus, alertness.
Body Language: Leaning forward, focused eye contact, nodding.

42. EXCITED
Definition: Feeling thrilled or full of anticipation.
Physical Sensations: Fast heartbeat, tingling in limbs, butterflies in stomach.
Body Language: Clapping hands, jumping, animated facial expressions.

43. EXCLUDED
Definition: Feeling left out or not included in a group or activity.
Physical Sensations: Heavy chest, cold limbs, tight throat.
Body Language: Looking down, arms crossed, turning away from others.

44. EXPOSED
Definition: Feeling vulnerable or lacking protection.
Physical Sensations: Tight chest, cold sweat, weak limbs.
Body Language: Crossing arms, pulling away, hunched shoulders.

45. FAILURE
Definition: Feeling inadequate or unsuccessful.
Physical Sensations: Tight chest, heaviness in limbs, weak breath.
Body Language: Slumped shoulders, downcast gaze, avoiding eye contact.

46. FEAR
Definition: A strong feeling of danger or threat.
Physical Sensations: Racing heart, cold sweat, rapid breath.
Body Language: Wide eyes, tense posture, trembling hands.

47. FEEBLE
Definition: Feeling physically or emotionally weak.
Physical Sensations: Weak muscles, shallow breath, low energy.
Body Language: Slumped posture, slow movements, soft voice.

48. FLOWING
Definition: Feeling natural, smooth, and unhindered in action.
Physical Sensations: Lightness, steady breath, relaxed muscles.
Body Language: Smooth movements, upright posture, calm expression.

49. FOCUSED
Definition: Feeling concentrated and attentive.
Physical Sensations: Steady breathing, strong heartbeat, heightened senses.
Body Language: Still posture, direct gaze, calm facial expression.

50. FRAGILE

Definition: Feeling emotionally or physically delicate or vulnerable.

Physical Sensations: Weak muscles, trembling, lightheadedness.

Body Language: Shaking hands, soft voice, protective body posture.

51. FRANTIC

Definition: Feeling overwhelmed and panicked.

Physical Sensations: Rapid breathing, increased heart rate, sweaty palms.

Body Language: Darting eyes, erratic movements, tense muscles.

52. FREE

Definition: Feeling unburdened and unconstrained.

Physical Sensations: Light breath, relaxed muscles, steady heart rate.

Body Language: Open arms, relaxed posture, smiling face.

53. FRUSTRATED

Definition: Feeling blocked or unable to achieve a goal.

Physical Sensations: Tight chest, clenched jaw, rapid heartbeat.

Body Language: Furrowed brows, tense posture, tapping or fidgeting.

54. FURY

Definition: Intense and uncontrolled anger.

Physical Sensations: Increased body heat, fast pulse, tight chest.

Body Language: Clenched fists, wide eyes, tense body.

55. GLOOMY

Definition: Feeling dark or pessimistic.

Physical Sensations: Heaviness in the chest, low energy, tense muscles.

Body Language: Frowning, downcast gaze, lack of movement.

56. GRATEFUL

Definition: Feeling thankful and appreciative.

Physical Sensations: Warm chest, soft breath, relaxed muscles.

Body Language: Smiling, open posture, relaxed shoulders.

57. GRIEF

Definition: Deep sorrow or sadness over loss.

Physical Sensations: Heavy chest, weak limbs, shallow breath.

Body Language: Slumped shoulders, tears, downcast gaze.

58. GRUDGING
Definition: Feeling resentful or reluctant.
Physical Sensations: Tight throat, clenched jaw, tense muscles.
Body Language: Crossed arms, narrowed eyes, rigid posture.

59. GUILTY
Definition: Feeling responsible for a wrong or mistake.
Physical Sensations: Sinking stomach, warm face, tight chest.
Body Language: Avoiding eye contact, hunched shoulders, downturned mouth.

60. HELPFUL
Definition: Feeling inclined to assist others.
Physical Sensations: Warm chest, steady breath, light energy.
Body Language: Open arms, soft gaze, leaning toward others.

61. HELPLESS
Definition: Feeling unable to act or improve a situation.
Physical Sensations: Weak limbs, shallow breath, heavy chest.
Body Language: Drooping shoulders, still posture, downcast eyes.

62. HOPEFUL
Definition: Feeling optimistic about a future outcome.
Physical Sensations: Lightness in the chest, deep breath, steady heart rate.
Body Language: Smiling, open posture, bright eyes.

63. HOPELESS
Definition: Feeling that no positive outcome is possible.
Physical Sensations: Heavy chest, low energy, weak muscles.
Body Language: Slumped shoulders, downturned mouth, vacant expression.

64. HUMBLE
Definition: Feeling modest or unassuming.
Physical Sensations: Light breath, steady heart rate, soft warmth.
Body Language: Lowered gaze, gentle smile, relaxed posture.

65. HUMILIATED
Definition: Feeling embarrassed or degraded.
Physical Sensations: Warm face, tight throat, sinking stomach.
Body Language: Covering face, looking away, avoiding eye contact.

66. HURT
Definition: Feeling emotional or physical pain.
Physical Sensations: Heavy chest, tight throat, trembling.
Body Language: Holding body, downcast eyes, stiff movements.

67. IMPORTANCE
Definition: Feeling that one's presence or contributions matter.
Physical Sensations: Warm chest, expanded breath, steady heart rate.
Body Language: Straight posture, calm expression, hands on hips.

68. INDIFFERENT
Definition: Feeling emotionally detached or uninterested.
Physical Sensations: Steady heartbeat, low energy, relaxed muscles.
Body Language: Flat expression, arms at sides, looking away.

69. INDIGNANT
Definition: Feeling anger over unfair treatment.
Physical Sensations: Tight chest, increased heart rate, clenched jaw.
Body Language: Crossed arms, raised eyebrows, direct eye contact.

70. INFERIOR
Definition: Feeling lesser in value or status.
Physical Sensations: Heavy chest, weak limbs, tight throat.
Body Language: Slouched posture, avoiding eye contact, downturned mouth.

71. INSECURE
Definition: Feeling uncertain or lacking confidence in oneself.
Physical Sensations: Tight chest, weak limbs, shallow breathing.
Body Language: Fidgeting, avoiding eye contact, crossing arms.

72. INSPIRED
Definition: Feeling motivated and creatively energized.
Physical Sensations: Light chest, steady heartbeat, warm limbs.
Body Language: Upright posture, bright eyes, animated gestures.

73. INTIMATE
Definition: Feeling emotionally or physically close to another person.
Physical Sensations: Warm chest, soft breath, steady heartbeat.
Body Language: Close proximity, soft gaze, relaxed posture.

74. INTIMIDATED
Definition: Feeling threatened or overpowered by someone or something.
Physical Sensations: Tight chest, shallow breathing, increased heart rate.
Body Language: Backing away, lowered gaze, tense shoulders.

75. ISOLATED
Definition: Feeling emotionally or physically separated from others.
Physical Sensations: Heavy chest, numbness, cold limbs.
Body Language: Looking down, folded arms, distancing from others.

76. JEALOUS
Definition: Feeling resentment or envy toward someone else's success or advantage.
Physical Sensations: Tight stomach, quickened pulse, shallow breath.
Body Language: Narrowed eyes, tight jaw, stiff posture.

77. JOY
Definition: A feeling of great happiness and delight.
Physical Sensations: Warm chest, light limbs, steady breath.
Body Language: Smiling, bright eyes, relaxed posture.

78. JUDGMENTAL
Definition: Feeling critical or disapproving toward someone or something.
Physical Sensations: Tight chest, narrowed gaze, shallow breath.
Body Language: Raised eyebrows, crossed arms, pursed lips.

79. LOATHING
Definition: Feeling intense dislike or disgust.
Physical Sensations: Tight chest, increased heart rate, nausea.
Body Language: Furrowed brows, curled lip, avoiding eye contact.

80. LONELY
Definition: Feeling emotionally or physically isolated from others.
Physical Sensations: Heavy chest, low energy, tight throat.
Body Language: Downcast gaze, crossed arms, slumped shoulders.

81. LOVING
Definition: Feeling deep affection or care for someone.
Physical Sensations: Warm chest, relaxed breathing, steady heartbeat.
Body Language: Soft eyes, open arms, relaxed posture.

82. MAD
Definition: Feeling angry or irritated.
Physical Sensations: Fast heartbeat, flushed face, tense muscles.
Body Language: Clenched fists, furrowed brows, crossed arms.

83. MEDITATIVE
Definition: Feeling calm and centered.
Physical Sensations: Slow heartbeat, steady breath, relaxed muscles.
Body Language: Closed eyes, relaxed posture, steady breathing.

84. MINDFUL
Definition: Feeling aware and present in the current moment.
Physical Sensations: Steady breath, calm heartbeat, soft muscles.
Body Language: Relaxed expression, soft gaze, still posture.

85. MOTIVATED
Definition: Feeling driven and determined to accomplish something.
Physical Sensations: Elevated heartbeat, increased energy, steady breath.
Body Language: Upright posture, focused gaze, purposeful movements.

86. OPTIMISTIC
Definition: Feeling hopeful and confident about the future.
Physical Sensations: Light chest, relaxed muscles, warm limbs.
Body Language: Upright posture, smiling, open gestures.

87. OVERWHELMED
Definition: Feeling emotionally or mentally overloaded.
Physical Sensations: Tight chest, rapid breath, weak limbs.
Body Language: Hands on face, furrowed brow, quick movements.

88. PANICKED
Definition: Feeling intense fear or distress.
Physical Sensations: Racing heart, shallow breath, cold sweat.
Body Language: Wide eyes, rapid movements, shaking hands.

89. PEACE
Definition: Feeling calm and harmonious.
Physical Sensations: Slow heartbeat, steady breath, relaxed muscles.
Body Language: Soft expression, still posture, relaxed shoulders.

90. PLAYFUL
Definition: Feeling lighthearted and fun-loving.
Physical Sensations: Light chest, quick breath, steady energy.
Body Language: Laughing, animated gestures, relaxed posture.

91. POSITIVE
Definition: Feeling confident and encouraged.
Physical Sensations: Steady heartbeat, warm chest, balanced breath.
Body Language: Upright stance, bright eyes, smiling face.

92. POWER
Definition: Feeling capable and influential.
Physical Sensations: Strong chest, steady breath, warm limbs.
Body Language: Strong stance, direct gaze, open arms.

93. POWERLESS
Definition: Feeling lacking in influence or ability.
Physical Sensations: Heavy limbs, weak breath, tight throat.
Body Language: Slumped posture, downcast eyes, closed body language.

94. PRESENT
Definition: Feeling aware and focused in the moment.
Physical Sensations: Steady breath, calm heartbeat, open chest.
Body Language: Direct gaze, open hands, still posture.

95. PRESSURED
Definition: Feeling stressed or burdened by expectations.
Physical Sensations: Tight chest, quick breath, tense muscles.
Body Language: Rigid posture, furrowed brows, tapping fingers.

96. PROUD
Definition: Feeling satisfied and honored by one's achievements.
Physical Sensations: Warm chest, steady heartbeat, light limbs.
Body Language: Upright stance, chin lifted, open gestures.

97. PROVOKED
Definition: Feeling pushed toward anger or aggression.
Physical Sensations: Tight chest, increased heart rate, tense jaw.
Body Language: Clenched fists, narrowed eyes, forward-leaning posture.

98. REJECTED

Definition: Feeling dismissed or unaccepted.
Physical Sensations: Heavy chest, cold limbs, tight throat.
Body Language: Downcast gaze, closed posture, avoiding others.

99. RELAXED

Definition: Feeling calm and free from tension.
Physical Sensations: Slow breath, soft muscles, warm limbs.
Body Language: Reclined posture, soft gaze, gentle smile.

100. REMORSEFUL

Definition: Feeling regretful or guilty for one's actions.
Physical Sensations: Heavy chest, tight throat, weak breath.
Body Language: Downcast eyes, slouched posture, avoiding eye contact.

101. RESPECTED

Definition: Feeling valued and acknowledged by others.
Physical Sensations: Warm chest, steady breath, soft muscles.
Body Language: Upright stance, direct eye contact, open posture.

102. RIDICULED

Definition: Feeling mocked or humiliated.
Physical Sensations: Warm face, tight throat, heavy chest.
Body Language: Looking away, shrinking posture, crossing arms.

103. RUSHED

Definition: Feeling hurried or pressured to meet a deadline.
Physical Sensations: Increased heart rate, shallow breath, tight chest.
Body Language: Quick movements, darting eyes, fidgeting.

104. SAD

Definition: Feeling sorrow or unhappiness.
Physical Sensations: Heavy chest, weak limbs, slow heartbeat.
Body Language: Slumped shoulders, downcast gaze, slow movements.

105. SATISFIED

Definition: Feeling content and fulfilled.
Physical Sensations: Warm chest, steady heartbeat, relaxed muscles.
Body Language: Gentle smile, open posture, steady gaze.

106. SCARED
Definition: Feeling fear or unease about a threat or danger.
Physical Sensations: Racing heart, cold sweat, tight chest.
Body Language: Wide eyes, trembling, quick movements.

107. SHOCKED
Definition: Feeling surprised, often in a negative way.
Physical Sensations: Rapid heartbeat, tense muscles, dry mouth.
Body Language: Wide eyes, open mouth, stiff posture.

108. SKEPTICAL
Definition: Feeling doubtful or questioning.
Physical Sensations: Tight chest, raised eyebrows, shallow breath.
Body Language: Furrowed brow, narrowed eyes, crossed arms.

109. SPONTANEOUS
Definition: Feeling free and impulsive without pre-planning.
Physical Sensations: Lightness, quickened pulse, high energy.
Body Language: Fast movements, animated gestures, bright eyes.

110. STRAINED
Definition: Feeling physically or emotionally stretched beyond capacity.
Physical Sensations: Tense muscles, shallow breath, low energy.
Body Language: Stiff movements, furrowed brow, strained facial expression.

111. STRESS
Definition: Feeling overwhelmed by pressure or demands.
Physical Sensations: Tight chest, quick breath, rapid heartbeat.
Body Language: Furrowed brow, tapping fingers, tight shoulders.

112. STRONG
Definition: Feeling capable and powerful.
Physical Sensations: Steady breath, expanded chest, energized limbs.
Body Language: Upright stance, open arms, steady gaze.

113. SUCCESSFUL
Definition: Feeling accomplished and recognized for achievements.
Physical Sensations: Warm chest, energized body, steady heartbeat.
Body Language: Open posture, relaxed face, steady eye contact.

114. THREATENED
Definition: Feeling endangered or at risk.
Physical Sensations: Fast heartbeat, tense muscles, rapid breathing.
Body Language: Wide eyes, defensive posture, darting gaze.

115. TIRED
Definition: Feeling physically or mentally exhausted.
Physical Sensations: Heavy limbs, low energy, slow heartbeat.
Body Language: Slumped posture, slow movements, drooping eyes.

116. TRUSTING
Definition: Feeling safe and confident in someone or something.
Physical Sensations: Warm chest, steady heartbeat, relaxed muscles.
Body Language: Open posture, direct gaze, soft smile.

117. UNFOCUSED
Definition: Feeling distracted and unable to concentrate.
Physical Sensations: Restless limbs, shallow breath, tight chest.
Body Language: Darting gaze, fidgeting, looking around.

118. UNMOTIVATED
Definition: Feeling lacking in drive or ambition.
Physical Sensations: Heavy limbs, low energy, shallow breath.
Body Language: Slouched posture, vacant expression, minimal movement.

119. VALUED
Definition: Feeling recognized and appreciated.
Physical Sensations: Warm chest, steady breath, light muscles.
Body Language: Relaxed posture, smiling, soft gaze.

120. VULNERABLE
Definition: Feeling emotionally or physically exposed.
Physical Sensations: Tight chest, weak limbs, shallow breath.
Body Language: Folded arms, avoiding eye contact, tense posture.

121. WHIMSICAL
Definition: Feeling playful and imaginative.
Physical Sensations: Light chest, quickened pulse, high energy.
Body Language: Animated gestures, bright eyes, smiling.

122. WITHDRAWN
Definition: Feeling emotionally or socially distant.
Physical Sensations: Heavy chest, low energy, slow breath.
Body Language: Looking away, crossed arms, downcast gaze.

123. WORRIED
Definition: Feeling concerned or uneasy about a possible problem.
Physical Sensations: Tight chest, fast heartbeat, shallow breath.
Body Language: Furrowed brow, biting nails, darting gaze.

124. WORTHY
Definition: Feeling deserving of respect and value.
Physical Sensations: Steady heartbeat, warm chest, relaxed muscles.
Body Language: Upright posture, direct eye contact, open arms.

APPENDIX 2:
Readers' Guide

'm delighted that you've picked up *Three Permissions*, a book designed to challenge, inspire, and even gently nudge you out of your comfort zone as you navigate your permissions journey. As with literal journeys, traveling with friends can support you on the way and make the road more fun with shared discoveries. This guide is here to help spark deep discussions, self-reflection, and maybe a few epiphanies along the way.

Each chapter in *Three Permissions* explores a different facet of giving yourself permission—to feel, to fail, and to fly. The following questions will help you connect the concepts to your own life, share insights with your group, and possibly uncover things about yourself that you never expected (don't worry, it's all part of the process!).

HOW TO USE THIS GUIDE

- Take Turns Leading: Rotate who asks questions to keep the conversation lively.
- Choose Your Questions: Pick a few questions from each section for your group to explore. Avoid group overwhelm by choosing a few that resonate.

- Be Honest: The best discussions happen when we drop the filters.
- Keep Confidence: Create a safe space to share without worry that your stories will be broadcasted.
- Stay Open: You might see parts of yourself in other people's stories.
- Have Fun: Be sensitive to serious moments in conversation but don't be afraid to notice the humorous aspects—laughter is encouraged!

PERMISSION TO FEEL

- What were you taught about emotions growing up? Were they welcomed or discouraged?
- When has suppressing an emotion come back to bite you later?
- How do you personally process emotions—do you lean toward avoidance, overreaction, or healthy acknowledgment?
- What have you noticed as you work to build emotional literacy?
- Of the four challenges, blame, self-trust, passivity, and identity, which is your greatest challenge?
- What's the difference between controlling emotions and partnering with them?
- Think of a time when an emotion actually helped you make a great decision. What was different about that experience?
- Where are you on the Permission to Feel Map? What is your current Permission to Feel goal?

PERMISSION TO FAIL

- How has your relationship with failure changed over the years?
- What's a past failure that felt devastating at the time but ended up leading to growth?
- What have you avoided something because you were afraid of failing? How did that choice impact you?
- What did you learn from your Failure Inventory? What advice did you give yourself?
- When has someone else's "failure" actually inspired you?
- What kind of learning happened in your Failure/Success Analysis?
- What would you attempt tomorrow if you truly didn't care about judgment?
- How can we create environments (at work, home, friendships) where failure is normalized and even celebrated?

PERMISSION TO FLY

- What's something you've always wanted to do but keep putting off? What's stopping you?
- What challenges do you face around dreaming?
- What did you learn about your beliefs and the rules you create?
- Share an example of when you achieved something great, only to feel unworthy of it afterward. What measures did you take to deal with those feelings?
- How do you personally handle success—do you embrace it, downplay it, or fear losing it?

- What habits or practices help you maintain momentum without burning out?
- How can you support others in their "permission to fly" moments?

CLOSING REFLECTION

- If you could share one thing you learned from *Three Permissions* with someone you care about, what would you share?
- If you could give yourself full permission in one area of life right now, what would it be?
- How do you want to show up differently after finishing this book?
- What's one way this group can continue to encourage each other after this conversation ends?

FINAL THOUGHTS

Growth is messy, failure is uncomfortable but important, and success is meant to be enjoyed—not feared. Keep giving yourself permission to feel, fail, and fly because how you show up has a ripple effect. Thanks for reading, reflecting, and being part of this journey!

Want to stay connected? Follow Robyn for more insights, encouragement, coaching opportunities and possibly an excessive amount of book recommendations.

Notes

Introduction

1. Joris Lammers, Janka I. Stoker, Adam D. Galinsky, "To Have Control Over or to Be Free from Others? The Desire for Power Reflects a Need for Autonomy," *Society for Personality and Social Psychology* 42, no. 4 (April 2016), https://doi.org/10.1177/0146167216634064. Julie Beck, "People Want Power Because They Want Autonomy," *The Atlantic*, accessed February 7, 2025, https://www.theatlantic.com/health/archive/2016/03/people-want-power-because-they-want-autonomy/474669/.

Chapter 1

1. Antonio Damasio, *Descartes' Error* (New York: Penguin Books, 2005).

Chapter 2

1. Olga Khazan, "Why Self-Compassion Works Better Than Self-Esteem," *The Atlantic*, accessed May 6, 2016, www.theatlantic.com/health/archive/2016/05/why-self-compassion-works-better-than-self-esteem/481473.
2. APA Dictionary of Psychology, "Passivity," accessed February 7, 2025, https://dictionary.apa.org/passivity.
3. Michael Hyatt, "How to Create More Margin in Your Life," *Full Focus Planner*, accessed February 7, 2025, https://fullfocusplanner.com/more-margin.

Chapter 5

1. YouTube, "Shining Like Stars in Deepening Darkness—Part 1 of 5," Living Proof Ministries with Beth Moore, accessed February 7, 2025, www.youtube.com/watch?v=oNlEO_GFTfs&t=12s.
2. James R. Bailey and Scheherazade Rehman, "Don't Underestimate the Power of Self-Reflection," *Harvard Business Review*, March 4, 2022, https://hbr.org/2022/03/dont-underestimate-the-power-of-self-reflection.

Part II

1. Meg Jones, "Apollo Flight Director Gene Kranz speaking in Oshkosh," *Milwaukee Journal Sentinel*, December 4, 2016, www.jsonline.com/story/news/local/wisconsin/2016/12/04/apollo-flight-director-gene-kranz-speaking-oshkosh/94312900.

Chapter 6

1. Dickens, Charles, *A Christmas Carol* (London: Chapman & Hall, 1843).
2. Brené Brown, *Daring Greatly: How the Courage to Be Vulnerable Transforms the Way We Live, Love, Parent, and Lead* (New York: Avery Publishing, 2015).
3. Carol Dweck, *Mindset* (New York: Ballantine Books, 2007).
4. Moheb Costandi, *Neuroplasticity* (Cambridge, MA: The MIT Press, 2016).

Chapter 7

1. Thomas Curran and Andrew P. Hill, "Perfectionism Is Increasing Over Time: A Meta-Analysis of Birth Cohort Differences From 1989 to 2016," *Psychological Bulletin* 145, no. 4 (2019): 410–429.
2. Stephen Guise, *How to Be an Imperfectionist* (Seattle, WA: Selective Entertainment LLC, 2015).
3. Costandi, *Neuroplasticity*.

Chapter 8

1. Yian Yin, Yang Wang, James A. Evans, and Dashun Wang, "Quantifying the Dynamics of Failure Across Science, Startups, and Security," *Nature*, no. 575 (2019) 190–194, https://doi.org/10.1038/s41586-019-1725-y.
2. Kellogg School of Management at Northwestern University, "Why Do Some People Succeed after Failing, While Others Continue to Flounder?" *Kellogg Insight,* accessed February 7, 2025, https://insight.kellogg.northwestern.edu/article/some-people-succeed-after-failing-others-flounder.
3. Yian Yin et al., "Quantifying the Dynamics of Failure."

Chapter 12

1. APA Dictionary of Psychology, "Self-Serving Bias," accessed February 12, 2024, https://dictionary.apa.org/self-serving-bias.
2. Stephen M.R. Covey, *The Speed of Trust: The One Thing that Changes Everything* (New York: Simon & Schuster, 2006).
3. Marilee Adams, *Change Your Questions, Change Your Life* (Oakland, CA: Berrett-Koehler Publishers: 2009), 57.
4. Doris Kearns Goodwin, *Team of Rivals* (New York: Penguin, 2009).
5. Kirsten Weir, "Feel Like a Fraud?" *American Psychological Association*, 2013, www.apa.org/gradpsych/2013/11/fraud.
6. Weir, "Feel Like a Fraud?"
7. "Do You Have an ANT Infestation in Your Head?" *Amen Clinics*, accessed September 16, 2020, www.amenclinics.com/blog/do-you-have-an-ant-infestation-in-your-head.
8. Mel Robbins, "The 'Let Them' Theory," TikTok, June 15, 2023, www.tiktok.com/@jadedmotivation/video/7244870208656051499?lang=en;. *The Mel Robbins Podcast*, episode 70, "The 'Let Them Theory': A Life-Changing Mindset Hack That 15 Million People Can't Stop Talking About," May 29, 2023.

Chapter 13

1. N.C. Ebner, A.M. Freund, and P.B. Baltes, "Developmental Changes in Personal Goal Orientation from Young to Late Adulthood: From Striving for Gains to Maintenance and Prevention of Losses," *Psychology and Aging* 4, no. 21 (December 2006): 664–678, https://doi.org/10.1037/0882-7974.21.4.664.
2. Ferris Jabr, "Cache Cab: Taxi Drivers' Brains Grow to Navigate London's Streets," *Scientific American*, accessed February 7, 2025, www.scientificamerican.com/article/london-taxi-memory.
3. "Reticular Activating System | Definition & Function," Study.com, accessed February 14, 2024, https://study.com/academy/lesson/reticular-activating-system-definition-function.html.

Chapter 14

1. Aircraft Performance Group, "Types of Flight Plans Explained," FlyAPG.com blog, accessed February 7, 2025, https://flyapg.com/blog/types-of-flight-plans-explained.
2. G.T. Doran, "There's a SMART Way to Write Management's Goals and Objectives," *Journal of Management Review* 70 (1981): 35–36.

Chapter 15

1. Carol S. Dweck, *Mindset: The New Psychology of Success* (New York: Ballantine Books, 2007), Chapter 1.

About the Author

Robyn White PCC, CPLC, is a certified professional coach, an adjunct faculty member at the University of Denver College of Professional Studies, the host of the *Boss Yourself First* podcast, and a passionate advocate for authentic self-leadership. With warmth, humor, and keen insight, Robyn guides individuals and teams to courageously give themselves permission to feel deeply, fail forward, and fly bravely.

Drawing from extensive experience as a coach and facilitator, Robyn teaches that true freedom and impact start when we embrace our challenges with compassion and authenticity.

Outside of her professional pursuits, Robyn enjoys diving into a good mystery novel, volunteering in her community, and savoring a perfect cup of tea. She lives in Colorado, enjoying family time with her husband of thirty-five years, their three daughters, one son-in-law, two grandsons, and beloved pets.

Robyn believes that self-leadership isn't about perfection—it's about showing up with courage, curiosity, and kindness, no matter what life brings.

www.ingramcontent.com/pod-product-compliance
Lightning Source LLC
Chambersburg PA
CBHW060516080526
44586CB00012B/509